DK EYEWITNESS TOP 10 TRAVEL GUIDES

VENICE

GILLIAN PRICE

D0620665

DK

DORLING KINDERSLEY
LONDON · NEW YORK · MUNICH
MELBOURNE · DELHI
WWW.DK.COM

Left **Piazza San Marco** Right **Façade, Doge's Palace**

A DORLING KINDERSLEY BOOK

www.dk.com

Produced by
Book Creation Services Ltd, London

Reproduced by Colourscan, Singapore
Printed and bound in Italy by
Graphicom

First published in Great Britain in
2002
by Dorling Kindersley Limited
80 Strand, London WC2R 0RL
A Penguin Company

ISBN 0 7513 3824 9

Within each Top 10 list in this book, no
hierarchy of quality or popularity is
implied. All 10 are, in the editor's
opinion, of roughly equal merit.

Contents

Venice's Top 10

**The information in this
DK Eyewitness Top 10 Travel Guide is checked regularly.**
Every effort has been made to ensure that this book is as up-to-date as possible at the time
of going to press. Some details, however, such as telephone numbers, opening hours,
prices, gallery hanging arrangements and travel information are liable to change. The
publishers cannot accept responsibility for any consequences arising from the use of this
book, nor for any material on third party websites, and cannot guarantee that any website
address in this book will be a suitable source of travel information. We value the views and
suggestions of our readers very highly. Please write to:
Senior Publishing Manager, DK Eyewitness Travel Guides,
Dorling Kindersley, 80 Strand, London WC2R 0RL.

Left **Ballroom, Museo Correr** Right **Gondola traghetto ride**

Left **Mercerie shops** Right **Venice Carnival**

VENICE'S
TOP 10

VENICE'S TOP 10

ᴛᴏᴘ10 Venice Highlights

The uniquely romantic city of Venice was built entirely on water and has managed to survive into the 21st century without cars. Narrow alleyways and canals pass between sumptuous palaces and magnificent churches, colourful neighbourhood markets and quiet backwaters, unchanged for centuries. Few cities possess such an awesome line-up of sights for visitors.

Basilica San Marco **1**

Venice's fairytale cathedral is pure Byzantine in essence, while its façade and interior have been embellished with resplendent mosaics and exquisite works of art through the ages *(see pp8–11)*.

2 Doge's Palace

This was the powerhouse of the city's rulers for nearly 900 years. Passing through a maze of rooms gives visitors an insight into the sumptuous lifestyle that so often accompanied state affairs *(see pp12–15)*.

3 Piazza San Marco

Elegance and opulence sit side by side in what Napoleon named "the drawing room of Europe". This magnificent square is adorned with monuments that give testimony to Venice's glorious past *(see pp16–19)*.

4 Grand Canal

The city's majestic watercourse swarms with all manner of boats, while its embankments boast a dazzling succession of palaces dating back as early as the 13th century *(see pp20–23)*.

Cannaregi

Canal Grande

Santa Croce

Dorsoduro

Peggy Guggenheim Collection
[...]y's leading [mu]seum for 20th-[ce]ntury European [an]d American art, [the] collection is [hou]sed in a one-floor [pa]lace on the Grand [Ca]nal (see pp34–5).

9 Campo Santa Margherita
A wonderful square, bustling with life day and night thanks to its market stalls and outdoor cafés. An added bonus is its many architectural styles (see pp32–3).

8 Island of Torcello
Escape the crowds in the city with a ferry ride over the vast expanse of the lagoon to this peaceful, lush island, the site of Venice's original settlement (see pp30–31).

7 Rialto Market
This Mediterranean fresh produce market has enlivened this quayside since medieval times and is arguably still the best market in the world (see pp28–9).

250 ⌐ yards ¬ 0 ⌐ metres ⌐ 250

Accademia Galleries
An unsurpassed collection of [Ve]netian paintings, with master[pi]eces by Titian, Bellini and [Gi]orgione. A must, not only for art [lo]vers (see pp24–5).

6 Santa Maria Gloriosa dei Frari
A Gothic interior with grandiose works of art lies in store behind this church's brick façade (see pp26–7).

For guided tours around Venice **See p136**

7

⭐ Basilica San Marco

This breathtaking Byzantine basilica, dominating Piazza San Marco (see pp16–19), was constructed in such ornate fashion for two reasons: as an embodiment of the Venetian Republic's power and as a fitting resting place f St Mark. Serving as the Doges' chapel, coronations, funerals and procession were held here, gloriously framed by more than 4,000 sq m (43,000 sq ft) o mosaics, eastern treasures and 500 columns dating from the 3rd century.

Basilica San Marco façade

🕐 Visit the basilica at dusk, when the rays of the setting sun beautifully light up the façade.

Binoculars are a great help for examining mosaics high up on the walls.

• Piazza San Marco
• Map Q5
• 041 522 52 05
• Open: Basilica 9:30am–5pm Mon–Sat, 2–5pm Sun; Museum and Loggia Cavalli Apr–Sep: 9:45am–5pm, Oct–Mar: 9:45am–4pm Mon–Sun; Pala d'Oro and Treasury Apr–Sep: 9:45am–5pm Mon–Sat, 2–5pm Sun & public hols; Oct–Mar: 9:45am–4pm Mon–Sat, 2–4pm Sun & public hols
• Admission: Basilica free; Museum €1.50; Pala d'Oro €1.50; Treasury €2.00
• No disabled access beyond ground floor

Top 10 Features

1. Western Façade
2. Atrium Mosaics
3. Flooring
4. Pala d'Oro
5. Ascension Dome
6. Pentecost Dome
7. Basilica Museum
8. Loggia dei Cavalli
9. The Tetrarchs
10. Treasury

1 Western Façade
A marvellous succession of domes, columns, arches and spires, interspersed with marble statues, screens and glittering mosaics, greets tourists in Piazza San Marco. The northernmost arch houses mosaics dating from the 13th century, which depict the basilica itself. Other mosaics are 17th- and 18th-century copies.

2 Atrium Mosaics
These glorious mosaics *(above)* of precious gold-leaf over glass tiles were created in the Byzantine tradition by expert craftsmen, and give detailed accounts of the Old Testament. The 13th-century cupola's concentric circles recount 24 episodes from *Genesis*, including the Creation and Adam and Eve.

3 Flooring
The paving is a mosai masterpiece of multi-coloured stones on uneve levels, evocative of the se Geometrical designs sit alongside animal shapes.

For more Venice churches See pp38–9

Pala d'Oro
4 The dazzling jewel-encrusted gold screen was commissioned in Constantinople in 976 but frequently added to at later dates. It boasts 250 panels bearing 1,927 authentic gems and *cloisonné* plaques.

Pentecost Dome
6 Probably the first dome of the basilica to be adorned with mosaics, it is illustrated with the descent of the Holy Ghost *(above)*, seen as a flame over the heads of the 12 Apostles.

Basilica Museum
7 Inside the fascinating museum are the famed quartet of horses crafted from bronze and covered in gold. Booty from the Fourth Crusade, these triumphal Graeco-Roman equine figures originally graced the Hippodrome in Constantinople. They have been restored to their former glory.

Loggia dei Cavalli
8 Replicas of the proud horses now in the museum stand on this wonderful balcony overlooking Piazza San Marco. Visitors can see the ancient lead gutter spouts, as well as clutches of columns, whose varied dimensions and decorative styles indicate their diverse origins.

Basilica Floorplan

The Tetrarchs
9 The inspiration for these red porphyry rock figures from 4th-century Egypt is unknown. They may represent Saracens who, scheming to make off with treasure, poisoned each other and ended up as stone.

Treasury
10 The basilica's glittering riches include precious chalices of rock crystal enamelled by medieval silver- and goldsmiths and reliquaries from Venice's eastern conquests, including parts of the True Cross.

Building the Basilica

Construction began on the first building in 829. However, during a revolt in 976, it was burned down and dismantled. The building we see today, a Greek cross layout surmounted by five domes, possibly modelled on the Church of the Holy Apostles in Constantinople, dates from 1071. The main architect is depicted over the central portal, biting his fingers in frustration over a building defect. The basilica became the city cathedral in 1807.

Ascension Dome
5 The central dome as a spectacular array of early 13th-century mosaics, depicting the New Testament. *Christ in Glory* is shown above depictions of the Virtues.

For more on Venice's San Marco district **See pp72–9**

Left **Museum horses** Centre left **Wall-slabs** Centre right **Altar columns** Right **Byzantine screens**

🔟 Basilica Architectural Features

1 Galleries
The airy catwalks over the body of the basilica reflect the eastern tradition of segregation in worship as they were exclusively for women. They are closed to visitors.

2 Stone Wall-slabs
Brick-faced until the 1100s, the walls were then covered with stone slabs from the East, sliced lengthways to produce a kaleidoscopic effect.

3 Romanesque Stone Carvings
The exquisite semi-circular stone carvings over the central doorway were executed between 1235–65 and still bear traces of their original colour.

4 The "Victory Bringer"
This revered Byzantine icon is given pride of place in the Madonna Nicopeia Chapel. Rumoured to have been executed by St Luke, it was carried into battle for its miraculous powers.

5 Baptistry
Aglow with 14th-century mosaic scenes of the life of St John, this is also home to the tomb of architect Sansovino *(see p45)*. Closed to visitors.

Basilica Floorplan

6 Zen Chapel
The sumptuous decoration in this small chapel was executed for the funeral of its namesake, Cardinal Zen, in 1521, in recognition of his gifts to the state. Closed to visitors.

7 Iconostasis
This elaborate screen separates the worship area of the chancel from the nave. Its eight columns are topped with Gothic-style statues of the Virgin and the Apostles, sculpted by the Delle Masegne brothers in 1394.

8 Byzantine Pierced Screen
Influenced by eastern architecture, delicate geometrical designs and lattice-work stone screens are featured on all three façades, in the atrium and loggia.

9 Porta dei Fiori
This doorway on the northern façade bears a 13th-century nativity scene surrounded by vines and Moorish arches.

10 Altar Columns
Four finely carved alabaster and marble columns support a canopy at the altar, beneath which lies the body of St Mark.

Porta dei Fiori

For more on Venice architects See p45

Venice's Top 10 Relics

1. Milk of the Virgin Mary, Basilica Treasury *(see p9)*
2. Blood of Christ, Basilica Treasury
3. Nail from the True Cross, Chiesa di San Pantalon *(see p39)*
4. Thorn from Christ's crown, Basilica Treasury
5. Body of St Mark, Basilica San Marco *(see pp8–9)*
6. Body of St Lucy, Chiesa di San Geremia
7. Three rocks used to stone St Stephen to death, Basilica Treasury
8. Skull of St John the Baptist, Basilica Treasury
9. Leg of St George, Basilica Treasury
10. Foot of St Catherine of Siena, Santi Giovanni e Paolo *(see p102)*

St Mark, Patron Saint of Venice

Although the well-loved saint of Byzantium, St Theodore, had been appointed protector of Venice by the Byzantine emperor, the fledgling republic felt in need of a saint of its own. In AD 828, two adroit Venetian merchants filched the body of St Mark from a monastery in Alexandria, ostensibly transporting it under layers of pork fat to conceal it from Muslim guards. The welcome in Venice was triumphant, and the story was recounted in countless paintings and mosaics. The remains, however, were mislaid for years, until an arm

Stealing St Mark's body

miraculously broke through a column in 1094 (marked by a small cross, left of the Altar of the Sacrament) in answer to a prayer. St Mark now rests in peace beneath the basilica's main altar. The ubiquitous winged lion representing St Mark could be found throughout the republic as the trademark of Venetian dominion: it is often shown with two paws in the sea and two on land, to symbolize the geography of Venice.

Medieval Venice, centred around Basilica San Marco

For more Venice churches See pp38–9

⛅10 Doge's Palace

A magnificent combination of Byzantine, Gothic and Renaissance architecture, the Palazzo Ducale (Doge's Palace) was the official residence of the 120 doges who ruled Venice from 697 to 1797. A fortress-like structure stood here in the 9th century, to be replaced by the elegant Gothic version seen today, despite a string of fires in the 1500s. Artists such as Titian, Tintoretto and Bellini vied with each other to embellish the palace with painting and sculpture, not to mention architects Antonio Rizzo and Pietro Lombardo, the latter responsible for the ornate inner western façade.

Doge's Palace façade

☕ A quiet modern café in the former stables on the ground floor serves snacks and drinks as gondolas glide past the glassed-in doorway.

🌀 Don't miss the Museo dell'Opera near the ticket office as it houses many original 14th-century façade capitals – those outside are mostly 19th-century copies.

- Piazza San Marco
- Map R5
- Open 9am–7pm daily (last admission 90 min before closing time); closed 1 Jan, 25 Dec
- Admission: €9.00 (combined city museums ticket)
- Secret Itineraries Tour: 041 522 49 51 (advance booking essential); 10am & 11:30am daily; Admission: €12.50 (includes palace)

Top 10 Features

1. Façade
2. Sala del Maggior Consiglio
3. Sala del Senato
4. Prisons
5. Ponte dei Sospiri
6. Scala d'Oro
7. Sala dello Scudo
8. Armoury
9. Porta della Carta
10. Doge's Apartments

1 Façade

Elegant twin façades face the piazzetta and the quayside. Pink-and-cream stonework and a loggia stand above an arcade of columns with 36 sculpted Istrian stone capitals.

2 Sala del Maggior Consiglio

The majestic Great Council Chamber is lined with canvases depicting Venetian victories and a cornice frieze of 76 doges – a black curtain represents traitor Marin Falier (see p15).

3 Sala del Senato

The Senate members who met in this lavish hall *(above)* were nobles entrusted with debating war, foreign affairs and trade with the Doge. Time was measured by two clocks – one with a 24-hour face, the other with zodiac signs.

 For more Venice palaces **See pp42–3**

Prisons
4 A fascinating maze of cells is linked by corridors and staircases on both sides of the canal. Famous inmate Casanova *(see p52)* made a dramatic escape across the roof in 1756. The "new prisons" were in use until the 1940s and feature poignant graffiti by internees.

Palace Guide
Rooms are labelled with explanatory panels in English and Italian and are spread over three floors and several wings. Follow the red arrows. Highly recommended is the Secret Itineraries Tour through chambers which were once used for administrative purposes and torture.

Sala dello Scudo
7 Enormous globes and painted wall maps showing the known world in 1762 make this room a must. The map of Eastern Asia traces Marco Polo's travels to China, complete with camels, rhinoceros and the mythical Uncharted Lands of the People Eaters.

Armoury
8 Fascinating, if spine-chilling, collection of beautifully crafted firearms, ceremonial weapons and suits of armour from East and West *(below)*. Among the war trophies is a Turkish standard brought back from the Battle of Lepanto (1571).

Ponte dei Sospiri
5 One of the world's most famous bridges, the "Bridge of Sighs" is an early 17th-century Baroque structure that crosses to the palace prisons. It would reputedly cause the condemned to "sigh" at their last glimpse of sky and sea.

Porta della Carta
9 The main entrance to the palace (now the visitors' exit) has a beautifully sculpted 1438 portal by the Bon family. It was named the "paper door" because edicts were posted here.

Scala d'Oro
6 The sumptuous Golden Staircase, so-called for its Classical stucco decorations in 24-carat gold-leaf framing frescoes, led guests of honour to the second floor. Designed by Sansovino *(see p45)*, it was later completed by Scarpagnino in 1559.

Doge's Apartments
10 The communicating rooms of the Doge's living quarters are furnished with rich brocades, impressive fireplaces, triumphal friezes, gilded ceilings and works of art.

Left *Paradise*, Tintoretto Centre **Wellhead** Right **Giants' Staircase**

Doge's Palace Art & Architecture

1 Paradise
Possibly the world's largest oil painting (1588–90), by Jacopo and Domenico Tintoretto, it is said to contain 800 figures (Sala del Maggior Consiglio).

2 Arcade Capital
Proclaimed the "most beautiful in Europe" by art critic John Ruskin, this eight-sided carved capital on the southwest corner shows the zodiac signs and planets in imaginative detail.

3 The Triumph of Venice
Dominating the Sala del Senato is Tintoretto's glorious work of propaganda (1580–84) showing allegorical and mythological figures proffering fruits of the sea to Venice.

4 Rape of Europe
Veronese's allegorical work (1580) in the Anticollegio shows Europe sitting on a bull, alias Jove, who is nuzzling her foot.

The Triumph of Venice, Tintoretto

5 Drunkenness of Noah
A powerful sculpture from the early 1400s adorns the façade's southeast corner. Noah, inebriated and half-naked before his sons, is intended to portray the weakness of man.

6 Central Balcony
This magnificent early 15th-century stone terrace, embellished with columns, spires and a host of saints, opens off the Sala del Maggior Consiglio with a breathtaking view of the lagoon.

7 Giants' Staircase
So-named for its two colossal statues of Mars and Neptune, which were sculpted by Sansovino in 1567 as symbols of Venice's power. Visiting dignitaries would ascend the marble-lined stairs to the palace.

8 Arco Foscari
This triumphal archway of pink-and-cream stone layers leading to the Giants' Staircase was commissioned by Doge Foscari in 1438.

9 Coronation of the Virgin
The faded but inspired remains of Guariento's fresco, discovered beneath Tintoretto's *Paradise*, are housed in a side room, with panels explaining the restoration techniques.

10 Wellheads
Elaborate 16th-century wellheads were constructed to drain water from the gutters to the central courtyard.

For more Venetian artists and architects **See pp44–5**

Top 10 Events in the Venetian Republic

1. Venice founded on 25 April (St Mark's Day, AD 421)

2. First doge, Paoluccio Anafesto, elected (697)

3. St Mark's body brought to Venice (828)

4. Ruthless siege of Constantinople (present-day Istanbul) during Fourth Crusade under Doge Enrico Dandolo (1204)

5. Venice loses 60 per cent of its population to the Black Death (1348)

6. Doge Marin Falier decapitated for conspiracy (1355)

7. Genoese defeated at Battle of Chioggia, leaving Venice to reign over the Adriatic and Mediterranean (1381)

8. Victory over Turks at Battle of Lepanto (1571)

9. After 25 years of war, Crete is lost to the Turks (1669)

10. Napoleon invades the Veneto, bringing about the fall of the Venetian Republic (1797)

The Extent of the Venetian Republic

In its earliest days, Venice was little more than a huddle of islands in the middle of a shallow marshy lagoon, settled by a band of refugees from the Veneto region. Yet over the centuries it developed into a mighty republic reaching south to the Mediterranean and north to the Alps, based on the concept of trade. Salt was stored in massive warehouses, there were dealings in exotic spices and wondrous fabrics from the East, crusades were organized and fitted out here and relics procured. Its main population probably never exceeded 160,000, however well beyond the walled port towns strung down the Dalmatian coast were far-flung outposts such as Crete and Cyprus. These dominions protected key passages in commerce with the Arabic countries. Westward across the Po plain, Venice's influence took in Treviso, Vicenza and Verona, extending all the way to Bergamo on the outskirts of Milan and the mighty Visconti dynasty.

A doctor during the Black Death

Marine Supremacy
The Republic's gaining of maritime power is celebrated in *The Victorious Return of Doge Andrea Contarini after Triumph in Chioggia* by Paolo Veronese (1525–88).

🔟 Piazza San Marco

Long the political and religious heart of Venice, it's hard to believe Piazza San Marco was once little more than a monastery garden crossed by a stream. The glittering basilica and Doge's Palace command the east side of the square, while other stately buildings along its borders have been the backdrop for magnificent processions celebrating victorious commanders, visiting dignitaries and festivals. The western end was remodelled by Napoleon, who wished to construct a royal palace here. Today the piazza continues to bustle, with elegant cafés, live orchestras, children feeding pigeons, costumed Carnival crowds – not to mention duck-boards when it floods.

Bas-relief, *Doge's Palace façade*

🍷 An after-dinner drink in the piazza on summer evenings is accompanied by free café orchestras.

🕐 The best time to appreciate the beauty of the square is early morning, when only the city sweepers are here.

- San Marco
- Map Q5
- Campanile: Open May–Sep: 9am–9pm, Oct–Apr: 9:30am–3:30pm (closed Jan); admission €4.00
- Caffè Florian: 041 520 56 41; open 10am–midnight Thu–Tue
- Museum Complex: Open Apr–Oct: 9am–7pm, Nov–Mar: 9am–5pm; admission €9.00 (city museums ticket)

Top 10 Sights

1. Basilica San Marco
2. Doge's Palace
3. Torre dell'Orologio
4. Campanile
5. Piazzetta
6. Columns of San Marco & San Teodoro
7. Piazzetta dei Leoncini
8. Procuratie Vecchie & Nuove
9. Caffè Florian
10. Giardinetti Reali

1 Basilica San Marco
See pp8–11.

2 Doge's Palace
See pp12–15.

3 Torre dell'Orologio
A marvel to behold, the Renaissance-style clock tower features two bronze moors *(right)* hammering out the hours on the upper terrace. At Epiphany and Ascension there is an hourly procession of clockwork Magi led by an angel. According to legend, the craftsmen were blinded to prevent them repeating the work.

4 Campanile
Incomparable views of the city and lagoon can be had by taking the elevator to the top of this 98.5-m (323-ft) bell tower. Erstwhile lighthouse, watch tower and torture chamber, it was masterfully rebuilt to its 16th-century design following its clamorous collapse in 1902.

Plan of Piazza San Marco

Museo Correr

Libreria Sansoviniana

Piazzetta
5 Once an inlet for boats and witness to the arrival of distinguished visitors during the Republic's heyday, this now fully paved mini square fronts the lagoon.

Caffè Florian
9 Reputedly Europe's first coffee house *(below)*, the premises still retain their 1720 wood-panelling, marble-topped tables and gilt-framed mirrors *(see p75)*.

Giardinetti Reali
10 These shady public gardens, created during the Napoleonic era, took the place of boatyards and grain stores, situated just behind the panoramic waterfront.

Columns of San Marco and San Teodoro
6 These two granite columns *(right)* with symbols of the saints were erected in 1172 by Nicolò Barattieri. Public executions were held here.

Piazzetta dei Leoncini
7 Site of a former vegetable market, a pair of lions *(leoni)* in red Verona stone have been crouching here since 1722.

Procuratie Vecchie and Nuove
8 These elegant 15th-century buildings were the residence of the Procurators, responsible for state administration.

Venice's Bells

Booming through the city, the five bells in the Campanile have marked Venice's rhythms for centuries. The Maleficio bell announced an execution, the Nona rang at midday, the Trottiera spurred on the nobles' horses for assemblies in the Doge's Palace and the Mezza Terza marked a session of the Senate. The Marangona still tolls at midnight.

Left **Libreria Sansoviniana staircase ceiling** Centre **Bellini Room** Right **Correr Ballroom**

ᴛᴏᴘ10 Highlights of the Museum

1 Biblioteca Marciana Ceiling

The ceiling vault of the opulent reading room *(sale monumentali)*, inside the Libreria Sansoviniana, collapsed in 1545 and its architect Sansovino imprisoned – he was released to complete the job at his own expense. Titian selected artists for the decorations; Veronese was awarded a gold chain for the best work.

2 Libreria Sansoviniana Staircase

Bedecked with gilt and stucco decorations by Alessandro Vittoria, the 16th-century staircase leads from a monumental entrance on the piazza to the halls of the old library.

3 Bellini Room

Works by the talented Bellini family are on display in Room 36 of the Pinacoteca: the poignant *Dead Christ Supported by Two Angels* (1453–5) by the best known, Giovanni; head of the family, Jacopo's *Crucifixion* (1450) and son Gentile's portrait of *Doge Giovanni Mocenigo* (1475).

4 Correr Ballroom

This showy Neo-Classical creation was built for Napoleon. It is now used for exhibitions.

5 Two Venetian Ladies

Carpaccio's masterpiece of well-dressed ladies (1500–10) is in Room 38 of the Museo Correr. First thought to depict courtesans, the women are, in fact, awaiting their menfolk's return from hunting.

6 Map of Venice

Pride of place in Room 32 of the Museo Correr goes to Jacopo de' Barbari's prospective map-layout of Venice (1497–1500), painstakingly engraved on six pear-wood panels.

7 Veneziano Paintings

This prolific Byzantine artist is featured in the Pinacoteca's Room 25, with glowing two-dimensional religious portraits (1290–1302).

8 Canova Statues

Foremost sculptor of his time, works by Antonio Canova (1767–1822) in the Museo Correr include his acclaimed statue *Daedalus and Icarus*.

9 Narwhal Tusk

Once prized as the horn of the fabled unicorn, this 1.6-m-long (5-ft) tusk from the rare whale has been superbly carved with Jesse's and Jesus's family tree (Room 40).

10 Crafts & Guilds

Wooden sandals 60 cm (2 ft) high, inlaid with mother-of-pearl, illustrate the stiff demands of 15th–17th-century fashions (Room 48).

Venus statue, Canova

For more Venice museums **See pp40–41**

Top 10 Historic Events in Piazza San Marco

1. Foundations of Doge's Palace laid (AD 814)
2. Construction of basilica started (828)
3. First bullfight held (1162)
4. Square paved with brick, herringbone-style (1267)
5. Square paved with volcanic trachyte blocks (1722–35)
6. Napoleon demolishes San Geminiano church to make way for Ala Napoleonica (1810)
7. Campanile crumbles to the ground (1902)
8. Record flood 1.94 m (6.4 ft) above sea level (4 November 1966)
9. Pink Floyd rock concert attracts 100,000 (1989)
10. Campanile stormed by separatists (1997)

The Acqua Alta
Being in a vulnerable position on the edge of the lagoon, Piazza San Marco has been flooded by high tides throughout its history.

Acqua Alta Flooding

Acqua Alta ("high water") has long been disruptive to the city between October and March. As warning sirens fill the air, people drag out their waterproof boots, shopkeepers rush to put up protective barriers and street-sweepers lay out duck-boards in low-lying spots. Venice and its lagoon are subject to the tides of the Adriatic Sea but flood levels are caused by the coincidence of low atmospheric pressure, strong sirocco winds from the south and natural high tides due to moon phases. Piazza San Marco is among the most vulnerable spots. The flood gates designed for the Lido sea entrances are held by many experts to be both useless and harmful to the lagoon, however there are plans for an elaborate drainage system on the piazza, dredging canals and raising paving levels.

Piazza San Marco's worst floods, November 1966

⁝10 Grand Canal

Venice's majestic "highway", the Canal Grande, is only one of the 177 canals flowing through the city, but at some 4 km (2.5 miles) in length, 30–70 m (98–230 ft) in width and averaging 4.5 m (15 ft) in depth, it certainly earns its name. Snaking its way through the city with a double curve, its banks are lined with exquisite palaces, while on its waters colourful flotillas of gondolas, ferries, taxi launches, high-speed police boats and barges groaning under loads of fresh produce, provide endless fascination. In 1818, when the water was cleaner, Lord Byron swam all the way down the Grand Canal from the Lido.

Fondaco dei Turchi façade

🍂 Grab the front seats on *vaporetto* line No. 1 for the trip of a lifetime.

To beat the crowds, either start out from Piazzale Roma heading towards San Marco late afternoon or evening, or take the reverse direction in the morning.

• The Grand Canal runs from Piazzale Roma, the bus terminal and car park area, to Piazza San Marco. It is navigable courtesy of ferries Nos. 1 (all stops) and 82 (main stops only).

1 Fondaco dei Turchi

With an exotic air and distinctive round arches, this Veneto-Byzantine building (1225) was the Turkish trade centre for 200 years. It is now the Natural History Museum *(see p64)*.

2 Ca' Pesaro

This colossal Baroque palace, decorated with diamond-point ashlar work, was the final creation of architect Longhena. Home to the city's modern art collections, it is beautifully floodlit at night *(see p41)*.

3 Rialto Bridge

One of the city's most familiar views, the striking 28-m (92-ft) span, 8-m (26-ft) high Istrian stone Ponte di Rialto *(below)* dates from 1588.

For more Venice bridges **See pp46–7**

4 Riva del Vin
A sunny quayside with a string of open-air restaurants, this is one of the few accessible banks of the Grand Canal. Barrels of wine *(vino)* used to be off-loaded here, hence the name.

5 Ca' Rezzonico
The finest feature of this imposing palace is its grandiose staircase. Today it is a museum of 18th-century Venice.

6 Accademia Bridge
The lovely wooden Ponte dell'Accademia, built in 1932 by the engineer Miozzi, was intended as a temporary measure until a more substantial structure was designed, but it is now a permanent fixture. It affords stunning views of the Grand Canal.

7 Ca' Dario
With an ornamental Renaissance façade studded with multicoloured stone medallions, this lopsided palace is supposedly cursed due to a number of misfortunes that have overtaken its various owners.

8 Santa Maria della Salute
Longhena's 17th-century masterpiece of sculpted whorls beneath a towering dome, this church commemorates the end of a devastating plague in the city *(see p38)*.

9 Punta della Dogana
The figure of Fortune stands atop the erstwhile customs house, doubling as a weather vane. This is where the Grand Canal joins St Mark's Basin and the lagoon.

10 Harry's Bar
Legendary watering hole of Ernest Hemingway, this is also where the Bellini apéritif was invented *(see p57)*. Opened in 1931 by Arrigo Cipriani, it was named after the American who funded the enterprise.

Wave-induced Damage

Damage to buildings caused by wash has worsened of late with the spiralling increase of motor-propelled craft. Waves provoked by all manner of boats eat into foundations of buildings set on the water's edge, as well as making life harder for the gondoliers. Speed limits aim to curb this: 7 kmph (4.5 mph) for private craft and 11 kmph (7 mph) for public waterbuses on the Grand Canal. Narrower canals mean 5 kmph (3 mph), whereas 20 kmph (12.5 mph) is the maximum on the lagoon.

Stonework damaged by waves

Left *Traghetto* on the Grand Canal Centre *Vaporetto* stop Right *Motonave* on the lagoon

🔟 Watercraft of Venice

1 Gondola
Most commonly seen transporting tourists, a larger version is also used for the cross-canal ferry *(see p135)*, while the smaller *gondolino* is a slender racing craft.

2 Vaporetto

Strictly speaking, this is the capacious rounded waterbus, now also seen in an "ecological" electric model. A slimmer *motoscafo* serves the outer runs and narrow canals with relatively low bridges.

Vaporetto

3 Sandolo
A slim lightweight boat perfectly suited to hunting and fishing in the shallow waters of the lagoon, not to mention racing. Painted black, these "imitation gondolas" can deceive tourists on the back canals.

4 Topo
The most common barge for transporting goods, it can be seen loaded with everything from washing machines to demi-johns, often with a live dog "figurehead" on the prow.

5 Sanpierota
This flat-bottomed rowing boat is named after the inhabitants of San Pietro in Volta in the southern lagoon *(see p117)*. Once used for transporting fish to Venice, nowadays it is fitted with an outboard motor and photogenic oblique sail.

6 Bragozzo

With a gently rounded prow and stern, this brightly coloured sailing boat was traditionally used for fishing by the inhabitants of Chioggia *(see p117)*.

7 Fire Boat
From their station near Ca' Foscari, the red launches are called both to deal with fires and to rescue submerged obstacles and crumbling façades.

8 Garbage Vessel
The city's hefty waste-collecting AMAV barges trundle over the lagoon with the day's rubbish, as well as carrying out environmental monitoring.

9 Ambulance and Police Launches
These modern craft attract plenty of attention as they roar down the canals – only the emergency categories are allowed to disregard the city's speed limits.

10 Car Ferry
These brand new giants convey all manner of motor vehicles from the Tronchetto to the Lido.

Top 10 Gondola Features

1. *Forcola* (rowlock)
2. *Ferro* (prow bracket)
3. *Hippocampus* (side ornament)
4. Night lamp
5. Bronze stern decoration
6. Ribbed oar
7. *Felze* (cabin)
8. Gondolier's foot rest
9. Gondolier's striped shirt
10. Gondolier's straw hat

Venice's Gondolas

The quintessential sleek Venetian gondola has been plying the city's canals since as early as the 11th century, although it did not take on its present graceful form until the late 1400s. Compared to a mere 405 gondolas on the waterways today, as many as 10,000 were in use in the late 19th century: bridges were once few and far between and gondolas acted as ferries between one island and another, a custom that continues to this day across the Grand Canal. A handful of gondola yards still construct the boats

Gondolier in traditional dress

as well as carrying out repairs, such as San Trovaso in Dorsoduro (see p89). It's a costly and complex craft – eight different types of wood are needed for a total of 280 pieces to put together the asymmetrical craft, 11 m (36 ft) in length and 1.42 m (4.5 ft) in width, at a cost approaching 25,000 euros. A gondola weighs more than 350 kg (770 lb), including a 30-kg (66-lb) ferro (iron bracket) on the prow, to offset the weight of the rower. Originally painted in bright colours, the black gondolas that you see today were decreed by the Senate to prevent excessive shows of wealth.

Gondola mooring post

Redentore Festival *(see p62)*

🔟 Accademia Galleries

A dazzling collection of masterpieces spanning the full development of Venetian art from Byzantine to Renaissance, Baroque and Rococo, the Gallerie dell'Accademia is Venice's equivalent of the Uffizi in Florence. Giovanni Battista Piazzetta started the collection in 1750 to serve as models for the art school; in 1807 it was boosted by Napoleon with the addition of works from suppressed churches. The same year the collection moved to its present premises, occupying three former religious establishments: the 12th–15th-century Scuola Grande di Santa Maria della Carità and its adjoining church, and a 12th-century monastery remodelled by Palladio in the 1500s. More recently, in the 1940s, Carlo Scarpa modernized the layout (see p45).

The Tempest
2 This enigmatic 1506 portrayal of a woman suckling her child is by Giorgione (Room 5). The overall impression is of figures and the dream-like, stormy landscape blended into one whole.

Accademia Galleries entrance

🕑 Read the helpful free information available in each room. They contain almost entirely the same text as the audio guide.

- Campo della Carità, Dorsoduro 1050
- Map L6
- 041 522 22 47
- Open 8:15am–2pm Mon, 8:15am–7:15pm Tue–Sun (later opening in summer); closed 1 Jan, 25 Apr, 1 May, 25 Dec
- Admission €6.00
- Quadreria Corridor: 041 522 22 47 (reservations essential); open 3pm & 4pm Tue, tours in Italian only; free

Top 10 Works

1. Enthroned Madonna
2. The Tempest
3. Supper in the House of Levi
4. Pietà
5. Meeting and Departure of the Betrothed Ursula and Ereo
6. Procession in St Mark's Square
7. Madonna dell'Arancio
8. Coronation of the Virgin
9. Portrait of a Gentleman
10. Portraits by Rosalba Carriera

Enthroned Madonna
1 Giovanni Bellini's gloriously inspirational altarpiece (1487), painted for the Church of San Giobbe, can be found in Room 2. The presence of St Roch and St Sebastian alongside the Virgin suggest the aftermath of the plague, while the angel musicians at her feet are a homage to San Giobbe, patron saint of music.

For more Venice museums and galleries **See pp40–41**

3 Supper in the House of Levi

The forceful canvas by Veronese (1573) occupies an entire wall of Room 10 (below) and caused controversy in its time. The church authorities, who commissioned it as "The Last Supper", were angered by the inclusion of "dogs, buffoons, drunken Germans, dwarfs and other such absurdities" – so Veronese changed the title.

4 Pietà

Titian's last work (1576) is unfinished but it is also considered his best (Room 10), imbued as it is with golden light and a piercing sense of anguish.

5 Meeting and Departure of the Betrothed Ursula and Ereo

Part of Carpaccio's magnificent narrative cycle (1495) about a Breton princess and an English prince can be seen in Room 21.

Gallery Floorplan

Bookshop

10 Portraits by Rosalba Carriera

As a female artist in demand by 18th-century high society, Carriera was a rarity for her time and these late-Baroque works in Room 17 (below) display the soft romantic pastels that became her trademark.

6 Procession in St Mark's Square

Part of Gentile Bellini's spectacular cycle (1496) of the St Mark's Day procession in 1444 is seen in Room 20.

7 La Madonna dell'Arancio

This exquisite work (1496–8) by Cima da Conegliano, painted for a Murano Franciscan church, is enlivened with partridges and plant life (Room 2).

8 Coronation of the Virgin

This resplendent polyptych (1350) by Venice's leading 14th-century artist, Paolo Veneziano, is the first work in Room 1. Flanking the sumptuous Byzantine-inspired centre are events from the life of Christ.

9 Portrait of a Gentleman

Lorenzo Lotto's sombre image of a melancholic man of means in his study (1528) is possibly a self portrait (Room 7). Lotto was known for work entailing psychological insights.

Gallery Guide

The vast gallery is organized in chronological order for the most part and the 24 rooms, labelled with roman numerals, are equipped with explanatory cards in English. The Quadreria corridor, a former storage area, is filled with masterpieces. Reached via a fine free-standing spiral staircase by Andrea Palladio, it is visited free of charge.

For more on Venice artists **See p44**

🔟 Santa Maria Gloriosa dei Frari

A masterpiece of Venetian Gothic ecclesiastical architecture, this cavernous 15th-century church for Franciscan friars took more than 100 years to complete, along with its "brother" SS Giovanni e Paolo (see p38), and a further 26 years for the consecration of the main altar. A wonderful series of art treasures is held within the deceptively gloomy interior, which is almost 100 m (330 ft) long and 50 m (165 ft) across, from priceless canvases by Titian and Bellini to tombs of doges and artists such as Canova.

Titian's monument

🍴 There are some great cafés and eateries in Campo dei Frari with views of the church.

👶 Youngsters will love the nativity scene with day-night lighting effects and moving figures at Christmas time.

• Campo dei Frari, San Polo
• Map L3
• 041 275 04 62
• Open 9am–6pm Mon–Sat, 1–6pm Sun; closed 1 Jan, Easter, 15 Aug, 24–26 & 31 Dec
• Admission €1.50

Top 10 Features

1. Assumption of the Virgin
2. Rood Screen
3. Choir Stalls
4. Madonna Enthroned with Saints
5. Campanile
6. Canova's Mausoleum
7. Monument to Doge Francesco Foscari
8. Statue of John the Baptist
9. Monument to Titian
10. Mausoleum of Doge Giovanni Pesaro

1 Assumption of the Virgin

Titian's glowing 1518 depiction of the triumphant ascent of Mary shows her robed in crimson accompanied by a semi-circle of saints, while the 12 Apostles are left gesticulating in wonderment below. This brilliant canvas on the high altar is the inevitable focus of the church.

2 Rood Screen

A beautifully carved blend of Renaissance and Gothic elements by Pietro Lombardo and Bartolomeo Bon (1475), the screen divides the worship area and nave *(below)*.

3 Choir Stalls

Unique for Venice, the original three tiers of 124 friars' seats deserve examination for their fascinating inlaid woodwork. Crafted by Marco Cozzi in 1468, they show the influence of northern European styles.

For more Venice churches **See pp38–9**

4 Madonna Enthroned with Saints

Tucked away in the sacristy, and still in its original engraved frame, is another delight for Bellini fans (1488). "It seems painted with molten gems," wrote Henry James of the triptych.

5 Campanile

The robust 14th-century bell tower set into the church's left transept is the second tallest in Venice.

Church Floorplan

10 Mausoleum of Doge Giovanni Pesaro

The monsters and black marble figures supporting the sarcophagus of this macabre Baroque monument prompted art critic John Ruskin to write "it seems impossible for false taste and base feeling to sink lower".

State Archives

The labyrinthine monastery and courtyards adjoining the church have been home to Venice's State Archives since the fall of the Republic. Its 300 rooms and approximately 70 km (43 miles) of shelves are loaded with precious records documenting the history of Venice right back to the 9th century, including the Golden Book register of the Venetian aristocracy. Scholars enter the building via the Oratorio di San Nicolò della Lattuga (1332), named after the miraculous recovery of a Procurator of San Marco thanks to the healing qualities of a lettuce (lattuga).

6 Canova's Mausoleum

This colossal monument, based on Canova's Neo-Classical design for Titian's tomb, which was never built, was a tribute by the sculptor's followers in 1822.

7 Monument to Doge Francesco Foscari

A fine Renaissance tribute to the man responsible for Venice's mainland expansion. Foscari was the subject of Lord Byron's *The Two Foscari*, turned into an opera by Verdi.

8 Statue of John the Baptist

The inspirational wood statue from 1450 *(left)*, created especially for the church by artist Donatello (1386–1466), stands in the Florentine chapel. The emaciated figure is particularly lifelike.

9 Monument to Titian

Titian was afforded special authorization for burial here after his death during the 1576 plague, although this sturdy mausoleum was not built for another 300 years.

Rialto Market

The commercial hub of Venice is as bustling today as it has always been – records tell of markets here since 1097. The area is also the city's historical heart and took its name from Rivoaltus, the high consolidated terrain that guaranteed early settlers flood-free premises. The majority of buildings, however, date from the 16th century, due to a fire which swept through Rialto in 1514. During Carnival the stall-holders don medieval costume to vie with each other for custom and only the new awnings and electronic cash registers let slip the modern world.

Fabbriche Nuove arcades

In addition to fresh fruit from the market, picnic supplies can be bought at the delicatessens and bakeries in the neighbourhood.

- San Polo
- Map P2
- Fresh produce market: 7:30am–1pm Mon–Sat; Pescheria: 7:30am–1pm Tue–Sat

1 Fresh Produce Market
A treat for the senses, with artistic piles of luscious peaches and cherries, thorny artichokes and red chicory from Treviso. Fruit, vegetables and fish tend to be strictly seasonal.

2 Pescheria
Writhing eels, soft-shelled crabs, huge swordfish and crimson-fleshed fresh tuna are among the stars of the 1907 Neo-Gothic fish market hall *(above)*, barely out of reach of the scavenging, screeching seagulls.

3 San Giacomo di Rialto
The oldest church in Venice claims to have a foundation set by a pious carpenter in the 5th century, although the present building is medieval. The Gothic portico and 24-hour clock are well worth a look.

For more on shopping in Venice **See p138**

4 Public Rostrum

New laws and names of criminals were announced atop this porphyry column, supported by a stone figure known as *il gobbo* (hunchback).

5 Palazzo dei Camerlenghi

This lop-sided 1525 palace *(right)* once imprisoned debtors on the ground floor, but the top floors were offices for the city treasurers *(camerlenghi)*.

6 Gondola Ferry

A must for every visitor is a trip on the *traghetto* ferry across the Grand Canal – one of only eight still in operation. Custom dictates that passengers should remain standing.

7 Banco Giro Arcade

Merchants gathered to do business deals outside the city's first bank set up in 1157, now a wine bar. The state abolished private institutions in 1585, profiting from the activity.

8 Ruga degli Orefici

This lovely covered passageway decorated with frescoes has been home to silversmiths, goldsmiths and silk traders since the 1300s.

10 Fabbriche Nuove

Uniformed *carabinieri* (police) patrol the elongated law courts edging the Grand Canal *(below)*. Designed in 1552–5 by Sansovino they are recognizable by their 25 plain arcades.

9 Grand Canal Views

The Erberia, right on the Grand Canal, makes a wonderful spot for boat-watching since the relocation of the wholesale market from here to Tronchetto in the 1990s.

Place Names

Rialto market's narrow alleyways carry names such as Orefici (goldsmiths), Pescaria (fishmongers) and Erberia (vegetables), because the same type of shops once stood together. Local eateries for market traders also had evocative names such as Scimia (Monkey) and Do Mori (Two Moors).

🔟 Torcello

Some of the most breathtaking Byzantine mosaics in the world, found in the lagoon's oldest building, the Torcello basilica, reward those who visit this laid-back island, a beautiful 40-minute ferry ride from northern Venice. From the 5th century, mainlanders fleeing invading Lombards and Huns ventured across tidal flats to found a settlement that grew to 20,000 and lasted 1,000 years. However few clues to the past remain, as the canals silted up, malaria decimated the population and the power base shifted to Venice once and for all. Today Torcello is home to a handful of gardeners and fishermen.

Santa Fosca façade

🕑 **Insect repellent is a must in summer as fierce mosquitoes have colonized the open lagoon.**

• Boat line No. 12 from the Fondamente Nuove via Murano and Burano
• Map H1
• Basilica di Santa Maria dell'Assunta: 041 270 2464; open Apr–Oct: 10:30am–5:30pm daily, Nov–Mar: 10am–5pm daily; admission €2.50
• Campanile: open Apr–Oct: 10:30am–5:30pm daily, Nov–Mar on special request; admission €2.00.
• Santa Fosca: 041 730 761; open for mass only.
• Museo dell'Estuario: 041 730 761; open Apr–Oct: 10:30am–5:30pm Tue–Sun, Nov–Mar: 10am–5pm Tue–Sun; closed public hols; admission €1.50.

Top 10 Sights

1. Basilica Exterior
2. Doomsday Mosaics
3. Apse Mosaics
4. Iconostasis
5. Paving
6. Campanile
7. Throne of Attila
8. Museo dell'Estuario
9. Santa Fosca
10. Locanda Cipriani

1 Basilica Exterior

A miraculous survivor, this striking cathedral was founded in 639 but underwent radical restructuring in 1008. It retains its Romanesque form, light brick walls and an arced 9th-century portico.

2 Doomsday Mosaics, Basilica

In these 12–13th-century marvels *(below)* the *Universal Judgment* is dramatically depicted in superbly restored scenes of devils, angels, wild beasts and fires.

3 Apse Mosaics, Basilica

This moving 13th-century mosaic shows the Virgin in a blue robe with gold fringing, cradling her radiant child in a gentle stance. Below are the 12 Apostles standing in a meadow of flowers.

4 Iconostasis, Basilica

Exquisite marble panels show peacocks drinking at the fountain of eternal life, diminutive lions posing under a tree of tendrils loaded with birds, while six columns support 15th-century paintings of the Apostles with the Virgin.

5 Paving, Basilica

In vivid swirls of colours, rivalling the flooring in Basilica San Marco, are brilliant 11th-century *tesserae* of stone and glass. Cubes, semi-circles and triangles are laid into square designs. The floor level was raised 30 cm (1 ft) during the basilica's reconstruction.

8 Museo dell'Estuario

An intriguing if modest collection of archaeological finds from the island and priceless treasures from the church, are housed in adjoining Gothic buildings *(above)*.

Attila the Hun

The "Scourge of God", otherwise known as the King of the Huns, ruled from AD 434–53 with an empire stretching from the Alps and the Baltic towards the Caspian Sea. As part of his campaign against the Roman Empire, Attila attacked the cities of Milan, Verona and Padua causing refugees to flee to Torcello. Burning the cathedral town of Aquileia gave him special satisfaction – his men raised a hill in Udine so he could enjoy the spectacle.

6 Campanile

The views from this simple 55-m (180-ft) bell tower range over the vast expanse of the lagoon, with its meandering canals and tidal flats, to the Adriatic Sea, Venice itself and even north to the Alps on a clear winter's day.

9 Santa Fosca

Alongside the basilica is this elegant church based on a Greek cross design, encircled by a five-sided portico with columns and carved capitals. The inside of the church is only open for religious functions.

7 Throne of Attila

By popular belief this marble armchair *(right)* was the throne of the king of the Huns, though historical sources claim it was for the island's magistrates.

10 Locanda Cipriani

A favourite of Ernest Hemingway, who stayed here in 1948, the quiet charm of this guesthouse has attracted VIPs since it opened in 1938 *(see p146)*.

Attila, barbaric
King of the Huns

🔟 Campo Santa Margherita

This cheery, picturesque square in the district of Dorsoduro is a hive of activi
day in, day out. It owes its name to the Christian martyr St Margaret of Antioch
possibly a fictitious figure but highly popular in medieval times. Patron saint
of expectant mothers, she is depicted in a niche on the square's northern wa
with her emblem, the dragon. The square's capacious form, exploited by loca
children on bicycles and in-line skates, is due to an ambitious enlargement
project in the 1800s which opened up the south end by filling in canals.

Scuola Grande dei Carmini façade

🍴 Numerous take-away pizza slice outlets and bars serving sandwiches *(tramezzini)* and rolls *(panini)* make for a cheap lunch, and allow for the kids to run around.

- Dorsoduro
- Map K5

Top 10 Sights

1. Ex Chiesa di Santa Margherita
2. Palazzo Foscolo-Corner
3. Scuole Grande dei Carmini
4. Calle del Forno
5. Casa dei Varoteri
6. Corte del Fondaco
7. Chiesa di Santa Maria dei Carmini
8. The "House of the Moor"
9. Rio Novo
10. Altana Terraces

1 Ex Chiesa di Santa Margherita

A writhing 14th-century dragon symbolizing the martyrdom of the saint enlivens the foot of the bell tower of the former church. It has been restored by the university as the Auditorium Santa Margherita.

2 Palazzo Foscolo-Corner

This beautiful palace *(below)* is virtually unchanged since the 1300s and instantly distinguishable by its deep overhanging eaves. A striking Byzantine-style lunette, bearing an inset with the family crest, tops the entrance portal.

3 Scuola Grande dei Carmini

Glorious rooms decorated with Tiepolo's masterpieces are highlights of this confraternity. The upstairs ceiling shows *St Simeon Stock Receiving the Scapular from the Virgin.*

For more on Venice's Dorsoduro district **See pp88–93**

4 Calle del Forno

An unusual series of medieval-style projections from a first-floor dwelling, partly held up by brick columns, is one of the features of this busy thoroughfare leading to Piazzale Roma and the bus terminal. The street is named after a long-gone bakery *(forno)*.

5 Casa dei Varoteri

A splendid *bas-relief* of the Virgin sheltering a group of tradesmen in adoration adorns the former tanners' guild dating from 1725. Because of its isolated position, it was once mistakenly thought to be the house of the city's executioner.

Rio Terrà dei Catecumeni, Dorsoduro

Rio Terrà

Rio is a common name for canal, while *terrà* means filled-in. Dating back to the 14th century, the practice of filling in waterways was particularly widespread in the 1800s to provide extra pedestrian space. Some would be covered over with a system of low-slung arches so as not to obstruct water flow, exemplified by Via Garibaldi in Castello *(see p102)*. Recent campaigns, however, have encouraged the reverse procedure, with Cannaregio's Rio della Crea re-opened.

6 Corte del Fondaco

A charming covered passageway leads through to this minor courtyard where curious low bricked-in arches indicate the former site of a 1700s flour store. The name *fondaco* or store derived from the Arabic *fonduq*.

7 Chiesa di Santa Maria dei Carmini

This richly adorned church happily survived Napoleon's suppression of the Carmelite order of monks in the adjoining monastery. Many of its 13th-century features are intact, such as the sculpted entrance porch.

8 The "House of the Moor"

Research has proved that Shakespeare's *Othello* was based on Cristoforo Moro, son of a noble family sent to govern the island of Cyprus from 1508. This house at No. 2615 is his former home.

9 Rio Novo

Excavated in 1932–3 to form a short cut from Piazzale Roma to the Grand Canal, the canal *(right)* has been closed to *vaporetti* since the 1990s, due to building damage.

10 Altana Terraces

These timber roof platforms were common in Venetian palaces and used by the ladies of the house for bleaching their hair, which they exposed to the sun through a crownless wide-brimmed hat. They are now used for washing and drying clothes, and partying on balmy summer evenings.

Peggy Guggenheim Collection

The delightfully spacious, light-filled Collezione Peggy Guggenheim is home to works by more than 200 contemporary artists representing powerful avant garde movements such as Cubism, Futurism and Surrealism. The landmark collection, put together by its far-sighted namesake, is housed in the 18th-century Palazzo Venier dei Leoni, known as the "unfinished palace" because of its one-storey construction. As well as the wonderful works of art on display inside the gallery, there is also a striking sculpture garden and the former home of Peggy Guggenheim to visit.

Palazzo Venier dei Leoni façade

🍴 Take a break on the café's shady verandah for a light snack or a meal.

☀ Watch the sun setting on the terrace directly on the Grand Canal during the late evening openings.

Fondamenta Venier dei Leoni, Dorsoduro 708 (2nd entrance Calle S Cristoforo, Dorsoduro 701)
• *Map D5*
• *041 240 54 11*
• *www.guggenheim-venice.it*
• *Open 10am–6pm Wed–Mon (Apr–Oct: until 10pm Sat); closed 25 Dec*
• *Admission charge €6.00*

Top 10 Works of Art

1. The Poet
2. Bird in Space
3. Attirement of the Bride
4. Empire of Light
5. Woman Walking
6. The Moon Woman
7. Magic Garden
8. Mobile
9. Angel of the City
10. Three Standing Figures

1 The Poet

A wonderful starting point is this portrait (1911) by legendary Spanish artist Pablo Picasso (1881–1973), from his early Cubist period. The figure is executed from a limited palette of ochre and dark browns *(below)*.

2 Bird in Space

This polished brass sculpture (1932–40) was once classified by US customs as a "stair-rail", thus subject to duty. Its creator was Romanian artist Constantin Brancusi (1876–1957).

3 Attirement of the Bride

This portrayal (1940) of a orange-robed bride assisted by mutant animals and humans *(above)*, is by Max Ernst (1891–1976). The German Surrealist was married to Guggenheim in the 1940s.

For more Venice art galleries See pp40–41

4 Empire of Light
Magical light effects see darkened trees and a house silhouetted by a street lamp against a contrasting daytime sky with fluffy clouds, in this work (1953–4) by René Magritte (1898–1967). The Belgian Surrealist was renowned for his eccentric subjects.

5 Woman Walking
This serene elongated form of a truncated female figure (1932), apparently inspired by Etruscan design, is the recognized trademark of the Swiss artist Alberto Giacometti (1901–66), a short-term participant in the Surrealist movement.

Key to floorplan

- ▨ Gallery
- ▨ Nasher Sculpture Garden

7 Magic Garden
A deliberately child-like, warmly textured piece (1926) by Paul Klee (1879–1940), with smeary shapes and sketched-in faces and buildings *(below)*, fulfils the artist's desire to be "as though newborn… to be almost primitive".

8 Mobile
This simple master-piece of movement (1941) by Alexander Calder (1898–1976), which gave its name to all mobiles, hangs in the atrium of Guggenheim's house and shifts delicately in the breeze.

6 The Moon Woman
This vibrant canvas (1942) starring a skeletal stick figure with an odd, pad-ded curve is an early work by Jackson Pollock (1912–56), pre-dating his famous "drip" technique.

9 Angel of the City
Set on steps leading to the terrace, this bronze horse and rider (1948) by Italian sculptor Marino Marini (1901–80) greet passing boats in an outstretched stance.

10 Three Standing Figures
Beautifully placed in the Nasher Sculpture Garden, these abstract sculptures (1953) by Henry Moore (1898–1986) were inspi-red by Italian bell towers.

Peggy Guggenheim
This colourful US expat-riate (1898–1979) and heir to a mining fortune first came to Europe in 1921, quickly fitting into Bohemian Paris. Resol-ving to "buy a picture a day", she amassed a contemporary art collec-tion which was exhibited in both London and New York, before she made Venice her home in 1947. She is fondly remembered by locals for her faithful dogs and for owning the city's last private gondola.

Guggenheim and dogs

Left **Getting around on the water** Right **Crumbling Venetian façade**

🔟 Frequently Asked Questions

1 Is Venice still sinking?
Theoretically, that all came to a halt when the industries in Marghera stopped pumping out groundwater. However, recent studies document both a rise in relative sea level, combined with accelerating subsidence due to changes in plate tectonics and soft sediments compacting under the weight of buildings.

2 What do the buildings stand on?
In the course of the city's history, millions of pinewood piles from the Republic's carefully cultivated forests in the Alps were driven deep into the compressed clay-mud base and, over time, petrified in the absence of oxygen. These were successively overlaid with horizontal planks and marble-like Istrian stone slabs which served as the foundations for buildings.

Venetian brick façade

3 Do people often fall in the water?
The odd tourist miscalculates the distance between the quayside and a waiting water taxi and takes the plunge – inevitably saved by timely intervention from a bystander. Be wary of moss-covered steps when taking a photograph or a rest and, of course, don't let young children out of your sight near water.

4 Why don't people restore the crumbling buildings?
Strict regulations concern façades – only porous stucco can be used for renovation as anything else tends to come away in sheets in damp, windy weather and is a hazard for passers-by. As a result, freshly plastered façades start crumbling weeks after application due to the high humidity and salt content in the air.

5 How deep is the lagoon?
At its maximum, 15 m (49 ft) in the navigable channels dredged for shipping and marked by bricole poles. Concern about the danger of silting and obstruction of the city's lifeline waterways has always been high – one preventitive measure was to re-route two rivers into the Adriatic Sea away from the lagoon. The Brenta was gradually modified between 1400–1600 to have it flow out after Chioggia, and the Sile was redirected towards Jesolo in the 1600s.

6 Does everyone have a boat?

On summer Sundays you would be forgiven for thinking that is the case, as families pack small craft with picnic supplies, sunshades, fishing or stereo gear and row, sail, punt or speed out across the lagoon. Many, of course, need boats for work. On average, one in two families possess a pleasure boat.

Private pleasure boats belonging to Venice residents

7 How many people actually live in Venice?

The 1997 census states 68,600, meaning figures have more than halved since the 1950s. Moreover, this includes Italy's highest percentage of senior citizens. Venice's permanent population is experiencing a slow but inexorable decline as young couples prefer to move to the mainland with the convenience of a car, not to mention lower house prices, cheaper shopping and fewer tourists.

8 Can you drink water from the drinking fountains?

Yes, it's the same as the tap water and subject to constant testing and treatment. Until 1884, when the supply piped from the mainland was inaugurated with a fountain in Piazza San Marco, the city depended on rainwater which was meticulously drained and collected in cisterns beneath squares equipped with locked covered wells.

Drinking fountain

9 How does the house numbering system work?

Within each of the city's six administrative districts (*sestiere*), numbers follow the alleyways along one side at a time, taking in branch streets and courtyards when encountered. In Cannaregio, the most extensive district, numbers reach 6420. The postmen are used to this confusing system, but visitors will need the name of the alley (*calle*), square (*campo*) or quayside (*fondamenta*).

Venice house number

10 Is the sea safe for swimming?

Yes. Periodic controls for bacterial counts are carried out and the upper Adriatic normally emerges with a clean slate. Venice's closest beach is at the Lido, where the city's families go en masse during the steamy summer months (see p115).

Left & centre left **S Maria G dei Frari** Centre right **Madonna dell'Orto** Right **S Maria dei Miracoli**

🔟 Venice Churches

1 Basilica San Marco
See pp8–11.

2 Santa Maria Gloriosa dei Frari
See pp26–7.

3 Santi Giovanni e Paolo
The monumental tombs of 25 doges take pride of place in this solemn Gothic giant, erected by Dominican friars from the 13th to 15th centuries. Among them is the grandiose tribute to Pietro Mocenigo for his valorous struggle to defend Venice's eastern colonies against the Turks (west wall). Inside are splendid paintings by Veronese and a polyptych (1465) by Giovanni Bellini.
◈ Campo SS Giovanni e Paolo, Castello • Map E3 • Open 7:30am–12:30pm, 3:30–7pm Mon–Sat, 3–6pm Sun • Free

4 Santa Maria dei Miracoli
A favourite among Venetians for weddings, Pietro Lombardo's showcase (1481–9) is resplendent again after restoration to deal with rising damp. The problem is not new – in Renaissance times marble slabs were affixed to the brick exterior with a cavity left for air flow. The ceiling gleams with gilt miniatures of holy figures *(see p95).*

5 San Zaccaria
An intricately decorated 15th-century façade by Coducci and, inside, Giovanni Bellini's superb *Madonna and Saints* (150? are highlights of this 9th-century church. The adjoining Benedictin convent, now a police station, used to host puppet shows to entertain the nuns. ◈ Campo S Zaccaria, Castello • Map F4 • Open 10am–noon, 4–6pm Mon–Sat • Free

6 San Giorgio Maggiore
Palladio's harmoniously proportioned church (1566–1610 inspired by Greek temple desigr stands majestic and isolated across the water from Piazza Sa Marco. The solemn interior is offset by two dynamic paintings by Tintoretto from 1594, *The Las Supper* and *Gathering the Manna* on the chancel walls. The bell tower offers views over Venice. Don't miss the monks' Gregoria chants every Sunday at 11am.
◈ Isola di S Giorgio Maggiore • Map F5 • Open 9:30am–12:30pm, 2:30–5pm dail • Admission charge (bell tower)

San Giorgio Maggiore

7 Santa Maria della Salute
A remarkable Baroque church dominating the southernmost entrance to the Grand Canal, its silhouette has become one of Venice's most wel known landmarks.

For more on Venice artists and architects **See pp44–5**

esigned by Longhena in 1630,
has a spacious, light-filled
nterior, while the altar houses a
recious Byzantine icon. Drama-
c works by Titian and Tintoretto
an be appreciated in the sacristy.
*Campo della Salute, Dorsoduro • Map
5 • Open 9am–noon, 3–5:30pm daily
(un–Sep: 6:30pm) • Admission charge
sacristy)*

8 San Sebastiano
Paolo Veronese spent a large
roportion of his life joyously
ecorating the ceiling, walls,
rgan doors and altar of this
nassuming 16th-century church,
nd was buried among his
olourful masterpieces, now
eautifully restored *(see p91)*.

9 Madonna dell'Orto
Huge canvases by devout
arishioner Tintoretto enhance
his graceful Gothic church set
n a quiet back canal. Two 1546
nasterpieces flank the high altar,
he gruesome *Last Judgment*
nd the soaring grandeur of *The
Worship of the Golden Calf*.
*Campo Madonna dell'Orto, Cannaregio
Map D1 • Open 10am–5pm Mon–Sat,
–5pm Sun • Admission charge*

an Pantalon

10 San Pantalon
Two treasures
lurk behind a
ramshackle
façade: a nail
from the True
Cross in a rich
Gothic altar
and the over-
whelming
ceiling by
ian Antonio Fumiani, a labour of
ove (1680–1704) which ended
vhen he purportedly plunged
rom the scaffolding to his death.
*Campo S Pantalon, Dorsoduro • Map
4 • Open 4–6pm Sun–Fri*

Top 10 Shrines and Tabernacles

1 Sottoportego de la Madonna
Pope Alexander III took refuge
here in 1177, in flight from
pirate Barbarossa. *Sant'
Aponal, S Polo • Map D3*

2 Gondolier's Shrine
A 1583 Madonna greets
boats approaching the bridge.
*Ponte della Paglia, S Marco
• Map R4*

3 Corte Nova
Painted images over a
lace-trimmed mantlepiece.
Castello • Map F3

4 Covered Passageway
The Virgin's protection has
been implored here against
plague and enemy attacks.
Calle Zorzi, Castello • Map F3

5 Scuola Grande della Misericordia
Carvings of laden boats invoke
protection for the ferries,
which set out from here.
Cannaregio • Map D2

6 Corte de Ca' Sarasina
Shrine dating back to the
1600s in memory of the dead.
Castello • Map F3

7 St Anthony
This 1668 "wardrobe" is
full of fresh flower offerings.
*Calle Larga, Cannaregio
• Map D2*

8 Ponte del Fontego
A Neo-Classical bridge
featuring gondola *bas-reliefs*.
*Campo S Giustina, Castello
• Map F3*

9 Gondola Traghetto Point
Madonna statue perched on a
pole in the Grand Canal.
S Tomà, S Polo • Map L4

10 Boatmen's Pole
Tabernacle midway on the
San Giuliano-Venice channel.

Left **Burano lacework** Centre **Museo Storico Navale** Right **Museo dell'Arte Vetrario**

🔟 Museums and Galleries

1 Accademia Galleries
See pp24–5.

2 Scuola Grande di San Rocco
The San Rocco confraternity has now been turned into a gallery to display its spectacular works by Tintoretto. The artist won the commission hands down – not content with a sketch, he completed an entire canvas. He then spent 23 years on the cycle of 60 inspired Old and New Testament scenes, culminating in the breathtaking *Crucifixion* (1565). They are the crowning glory of Tintoretto's life work *(see p81)*.

3 Fondazione Querini Stampalia
This unmissable Renaissance palace was the bequest of Giovanni Querini in 1868, the last member of the illustrious dynasty, on the condition that the library be made available "particularly in the evenings for the convenience of scholars". The immaculately restored palace-museum houses fascinating scenes of public and private life by Gabriel Bella and Pietro Longhi, as well as Carlo Scarpa's Modernist creations.
🔇 Campo S Maria Formosa, Castello 5252 • Map E3 • Open 10am–1pm, 3–6pm Tue–Sun (Fri & Sat until 10pm) • Admission charge

4 Museo dell'Arte Vetrario
A phenomenal chandelier from 1864, constructed from 356 handmade pieces, weighing 330 kg (730 lb) and measuring nearly 7 m (23 ft) in circumferenc[e] and 4 m (13 ft) high, is the star of this glass museum in the Palazzo Giustiniani. Other exhibit[s] include Phoenician phials, blown vases, ruby chalices, exquisite mirrors and the famed kaleidoscopic beads once traded world wide. 🔇 Fondamenta Giustiniani 8, Murano • Map G1 • Open Apr–Oct: 10am–5pm Thu–Tue (Nov–Mar: 10am– 4pm) • Admission charge

5 Museo Correr
Priceless artworks and a miscellany of items on Venice's history are housed in this fine museum on Piazza San Marco *(see pp18–19)*.

6 Scuola di San Giorgio degli Schiavoni
The finest work of Vittorio Carpaccio can be seen at the confra[] ternity of the Slavs *(Schiavoni)*.

Fondazione Querini Stampalia

laying the dragon is one of the
cenes from the lives of Dalma-
an saints, executed in 1502.
Calle dei Furlani, Castello 3259 • Map
4 • Open Apr–Oct: 9:30am–12:30pm,
:30–6:30pm Tue–Sun (Nov–Mar: 10am–
2:30pm, 3–6pm) • Admission charge

7 Museo Storico Navale

Watercraft galore are on
isplay at the Historic
Naval Museum, but
he highlight is the
eplica of the Doge's
eremonial barge
Bucintoro, richly
decorated with
llegorical statues.
Campo S Biagio, Castello
148 • Map G4 • Open
:45am–1pm daily
Admission charge

8 Ca' Pesaro Galleria d'Arte Moderna

A Baroque triumph of
a palace whose interior, in
contrast, accommodates works
by leading European 19th- and
20th-century masters such as
Marc Chagall and Gustave Klimt.
Fondamenta Ca' Pesaro, S Croce 2076
• Map N1 • Closed for restructuring until
2003

9 Museo del Merletto

A must for crafts enthusiasts
is the lacemaking island of
Burano and this precious display
of more than 200 rare lace items,
documenting a 500-year history.
Piazza Baldassare Galuppi, Burano
• Map H1 • Open Apr–Oct: 10am–5pm
daily; Nov–Feb: 10am–4pm Wed–Mon
• Admission charge

Studio with a Fruit Bowl (1942), Raoul Dufy, Ca' Pesaro

10 Museo di Icone

A rich collection of 14th–
18th-century Byzantine icons is
on display here, brought by refugees or painted by Greek artists
living in Venice. Ponte dei Greci,
Castello 3412 • Map F4 • Open 10am–
5pm daily • Admission charge

Left **Ca' d'Oro** Centre **Ca' Foscari** Right **Ca' Dario**

🔟 Venice Palaces

1 Doge's Palace
See pp12–15.

2 Ca' d'Oro
The original lapis-lazuli, vermilion and gold façade has long faded, but the breathtaking Gothic delicacy of this "golden palace" is intact, with exquisite marble tracery and arcaded loggias crafted by 15th-century stonemasons *(see p95).*

3 Ca' Foscari
Set on a strategic bend of the Grand Canal, this excellent example of late Gothic architecture has a series of mullioned windows facing the water, surmounted by an Istrian stone frieze. Once home to the long-ruling Doge Francesco Foscari, today it is part of the University of Venice. ⊗ *Calle Foscari, Dorsoduro 3932 • Map L5 • Closed to public*

4 Palazzo Vendramin-Calergi
This stately Renaissance residence by architects Lombardo and Coducci was home to a string of noble families including the Cretan merchant Calergi in 1589. Another famed tenant was German composer Richard Wagner, who spent his final years here. The palace is now home to the glittering City Casino *(see p60).*

5 Ca' Dario
Framed multicoloured round stones *(tondi)* embellish this privately owned asymmetrical palace dating from 1486. It was built for Giovanni Dario, ambassador to Constantinople, where he negotiated a peace treaty bringing long-term hostilities between Venice and the Turks to a temporary halt *(see p21).*

6 Ca' Rezzonico
This glittering palace adorned with Tiepolo ceiling frescoes, majestic Murano glass chandelier and elaborate carved period furniture, has undergone extensive renovation. It is now home to the Museum of 18th-century Venetian Life. ⊗ *Fondamenta Rezzonico, Dorsoduro 3136 • Map L5 • Open 10am–6pm Wed–Mon • Admission charge*

7 Palazzo Mastelli
This eclectic delight, tucked away on a peaceful back canal of Cannaregio, was the abode of three merchant brothers from

Palazzo Vendramin-Calergi

Morea on the Peloponnese from
112. Their turbaned likenesses
n stone adorn neighbouring
ampo dei Mori *(see p95)*. A
ascinating carved menagerie of
ons, birds and a prominent
amel can be picked out on the
Gothic façade. ◈ *Rio della Madonna
ell'Orto, Cannaregio 3932 • Map D1
Closed to public*

8 Palazzi Contarini degli Scrigni

15th-century residence,
nlarged by architect Vincenzo
camozzi for the 17th-century
roprietor Contarini "of the
offers" *(scrigni)*, so-called for
he vast wealth of his family
which resided in the Veneto
egion. The roof-top "folly" acted
s a useful observatory for
stronomers. ◈ *Calle Contarini Corfu,
Dorsoduro 1057 • Map B5 • Closed to
ublic*

9 Palazzi Barbaro

Cole Porter, Diaghilev, Monet
nd Whistler are just a few of
he great names who figure
mong the past guests of this
rivate double palace, courtesy
f the 19th-century Curtis family
rom Boston. Henry James
wrote *The Aspen Papers* here
nd used it as the setting for *The
Wings of a Dove (see p51)*. ◈ *Rio
ell'Orso, S Marco 2840 • Map P5
Closed to public*

10 Palazzo Pisani-Moretta

Venue of a fabulous masked
all during Carnival, when VIP
uests still glide up in gondolas
o the candlelit Gothic façade on
he Grand Canal, as did the Tsar
f Russia and Napoleon's Jose-
hine in days gone by. Tiepolo
nd Guarana contributed to the
nterior Baroque decorations.
◈ *Ramo Pisani e Barbarigo, S Polo 2766 •
Map N3 • Open for private functions only*

Top 10 Architectural Features of a Palazzo

1 Piano nobile
The high-ceilinged first floor of a palazzo hosts the sumptuous salons and family's living quarters.

2 Façade
Usually fronting a canal, this was the only exterior wall decorated with a costly stone overlay to impress visitors.

3 Funnel-shaped Chimneys
These and many other variations punctuate rooftops, their long shafts often running along outside walls.

4 Kitchen
This was always located on the ground floor for practical reasons.

5 Canal Entrance
Where the family's private gondolas were moored and visitors were received.

6 Central Well
This received filtered rain water for the palazzo's main water supply.

7 Entrance Portal
The importance of the main entrance was usually indicated by the distinctive family crest.

8 Enclosed Courtyard
This bustling area, usually with store rooms, was often used for the family's business transactions.

9 Altana Roof Terrace-Platform
These open-air areas were traditionally used for hanging out the washing or bleaching hair in the sun.

10 Land Access
With private gondolas, this was relatively unimpor-tant, hence a narrow alley.

Left **Giovanni Bellini** Centre *Mary with Child* (1511–12), Giovanni Bellini Right **Titian self-portra**

🔟 Artists in Venice

1 Giovanni Bellini
With his father Jacopo and brother Gentile, Giovanni (1430–1516) made Venice one of the greatest centres of Renaissance art. His trademarks are radiant Madonnas and serene St Peters.

2 Titian (Tiziano Vecellio)
A native of the Cadore region, whose Dolomite peaks often feature in his highly coloured works, Titian (1488–1576) studied under Giovanni Bellini.

3 Jacopo Tintoretto
The great Mannerist of the late Renaissance, Tintoretto (1518–94) produced huge, glowing canvases, seen at the Scuola Grande di San Rocco *(see p81)*.

4 Canaletto (Antonio Canal)
Famous for his landscapes of Venice and England, Canaletto (1697–1768) thrived under the patronage of the British consul Joseph Smith.

5 Paolo Veronese
Foremost painter of the Venetian School, Veronese's (1528–88) huge canvases, teeming with people, are on display in the Doge's Palace *(see pp12–15)*.

6 Giambattista Tiepolo
Tiepolo (1696–1770) is admired for his luminous poetic frescoes from the Rococo period, such as thos in the Scuola Grande dei Carmi in Dorsoduro *(see p28)*.

7 Vittorio Carpaccio
This Renaissance master (1465–1525) delighted in detaile scenes of daily Venetian life. Hi narrative style and command of light characterize his cycles.

8 Giorgione
Despite his brief life, Giorgione (1477–1510) produced memorable mood works, surpassing his master, Giovanni Bellini

9 Pietro Longhi
Longhi's (1702–85) witty scenes of the well-to-do in Venice can be admired at Ca' Rezzonico *(see p42)*.

10 Francesco Guardi
A prolific landscape painter, Guardi (1712–93) successfully captured the light and atmosphere of Venice in decline.

Rio dei Mendicanti (c.1723), Canaletto

 For writers and Venice **See pp50–51**

Left **Libreria San Marco, Sansovino** Right **Il Redentore, Palladio**

🔟 Venice Architects

1 Jacopo Sansovino
Trained in Florence under sculptor Andrea Sansovino, whose name he adopted in homage, Jacopo (1486–1570) fled to Venice to escape the sacking of Rome. Of his outstanding architecture are the Libreria and Zecca (see pp16–19).

2 Andrea Palladio
Regarded as one of the most influential architects of the western world, Palladio (1508–80) designed many Classical villas in the Veneto, along with the churches of Redentore and San Giorgio Maggiore in Venice.

3 Baldassare Longhena
The majestic Santa Maria della Salute, designed at the age of 26, is Longhena's (1598–1682) masterpiece, but his flamboyant style is recognizable in numerous churches and palaces, notably Ca' Rezzonico (see p42).

4 Pietro Lombardo
A native of Lombardy, sculptor Pietro (1435–1515) took over as director of works at the Doge's Palace when Antonio Rizzo fled, accused of embezzlement. His trademark is a leafy *bas-relief* pattern, also seen on his Renaissance masterpiece, Santa Maria dei Miracoli (see p95).

5 Mauro Coducci
The Renaissance designs of Lombard native Coducci (c.1440–1504) can be seen in the shape of Palazzo Vendramin-Calergi (see p60) and the churches of San Zaccaria and San Michele.

6 Bartolomeo Bon
Gothic sculptor and architect Bon's (1374–1464) designs were the basis for the church and Scuola di San Rocco. With his son Giovanni, he was also responsible for the Ca' d'Oro (see p42).

7 Michele Sanmicheli
Original military fortification designs by this Mannerist architect (1484–1559) are to be found on the former Venetian islands of Crete and Cyprus, as well as monumental portals in his home town Verona (see p124).

8 Antonio Da Ponte
Renowned for the landmark Rialto bridge (see p28), this engineer and architect (1512–95) also made numerous contributions to the Doge's Palace (see p12–15).

9 Giannantonio Selva
In Venice, French-inspired Selva (1757–1819) is best remembered for the elegant Fenice theatre, though he also played a hand in works of the Napoleonic era including restructuring the Accademia Galleries.

10 Carlo Scarpa
Modernist Scarpa (1906–78) admirably reorganized both the Accademia collection and the Querini Stampalia along Japanese-inspired lines.

For Venice churches **See pp38–9**

Left **Ponte degli Scalzi** Centre **Rialto Bridge** Right **Ponte dei Pugni**

🔟 Bridges

1 Bridge of Sighs
This evocatively named bridge once led convicts from the Doge's Palace to the adjacent prisons *(see p13)*. ◈ Map R5

2 Rialto Bridge
The design of this most famous Venetian bridge at the narrowest point of the Grand Canal was hotly contested – leading 16th-century architects Michelangelo, Sansovino and Palladio all entered the competition, but lost out to the imposing winning project of 1588–91 by Antonio da Ponte. There were two previous bridges on this site; a timber bridge which collapsed in 1444 under the weight of a crowd, then a drawbridge, raised for the passage of tall-masted sailing ships *(see p28)*. ◈ Map P3

3 Ponte degli Scalzi
One of the city's most marvellous lookout points, over fascinating palaces and boats, can be had from this elegant 40-m (130-ft) long bridge,

7 m (23 ft) above the Grand Canal. Named after the nearby monastery of bare-footed monks, this 1934 structure in Istrian stone by Eugenio Miozzi replaced an Austrian-built iron bridge. ◈ Map J1

4 Ponte della Libertà
Truth and irony combine in the name of this 3.6-km (2-mile) "Bridge of Freedom": the first full link between the mainland and Venice was put in place in 1933, when Italy was living under Fascism. The construction was preceded 86 years earlier by the Austrian-built railway bridge across the lagoon. Before that, the city relied entirely on boats. ◈ Map A2

5 Ponte dei Tre Archi
A favourite subject for artists, this unusual three-arched high bridge dating from 1688 crosses the Cannaregio canal close to where it joins the lagoon. It was the work of engineer Andrea Tirali, nicknamed Tiranno (the tyrant) by his employees. ◈ Map B1

Tre Ponti, Santa Croce

For getting around Venice by boat **See p135**

6 Ponte dei Pugni

Fistfights *(pugni)* between rival clans took place here until 1705 when they were outlawed for their violence *(see p90)*. Stone footprints marked the starting point of the combat, but contestants usually ended up in the canal. ◈ *Map D2*

7 Ponte delle Tette

When an increase in the practice of sodomy was recorded in the 1400s, the city's prostitutes were encouraged to display their feminine wares at the windows over the "Bridge of Breasts". ◈ *Map M2*

8 Bridge with No Parapet

One of only two remaining bridges with no side protection, this one spans a quiet side canal in Cannaregio. The other is the Ponte del Diavolo on Torcello. ◈ *Map N1*

9 Tre Ponti

Not three but five interlocking bridges span the Rio Nuovo canal near Piazzale Roma. The timber and stone structures afford views taking in 13 other bridges. ◈ *Map B3*

10 Ponte Lungo

Marvellous views of Piazza San Marco should entice visitors to this 33-m (110-ft) long iron bridge. Halfway along Giudecca, from 1340 it served as a link with newly reclaimed tidal flats. ◈ *Map C6*

Bridge with No Parapet

Left **Parco Savorgnan** Centre **Cloister of Sant'Apollonia** Right **Campo della Maddalena**

Hidden Venice

1 Parco Savorgnan

A well-hidden haven of chirping birds in towering shady trees, signposted from Campo San Geremia and Fondamenta Savorgnan. Part of the park once belonged to Palazzo Savorgnan, now a school, which backs on to it, and boasted statues, citrus trees and Roman stonework.
◎ Cannaregio • Map B2

2 Rio Terrà Rampani

This quiet thoroughfare, around the corner from Ponte delle Tette, is usually referred to as the "Carampane" (Ca' Rampani), alias the red-light district as of 1421. Venice had some 11,600 officially registered courtesans in the 1500s. A particularly narrow alley, Calle della Raffineria, site of a 1713 sugar refinery, runs off it.
◎ S Polo • Map M2

Rio Terrà Rampani

3 Corte del Duca Sforza

A picturesque courtyard opening onto the Grand Canal, i was named after the duke of Milan who took over a partially constructed palace here in 1461 However, work did not go much further than the diamond-point ashlar on the façade. The artist Titian used it as a studio when working on the Doge's Palace.
◎ S Marco • Map L6

4 Celestia to Bacini

A lengthy atmospheric walk way in a somewhat neglected zone of Castello, fronting the lagoon. The path clings to the wall of the ancient Arsenale ship yards (see p101), and leads to a cluster of workers' dwellings.
◎ Castello • Map G3

5 Corte dell'Anatomia

This quiet courtyard took its name from the anatomy theatre which existed here as of 1368. I 1671, a College of Anatomy was also established over the bridge in Campo San Giacomo dell'Orio, now an isolated building with a pretty vine-covered trellis.
◎ S Croce • Map L2

6 Campiello del Remer

This delightful square faces the Grand Canal and took its nam from the local oarmakers. It boasts several Byzantine features notably the wellhead of Verona stone and pointed ogee arches from a 13th-century palace.
◎ Cannaregio • Map P6

7 Cloister of Sant'Apollonia
Venice's only authentic Romanesque cloister has a court-yard with twin-columned arcades, now part of a church museum.
⊗ *Castello • Map F4*

8 Campo della Celestia
Now a tranquil residential square, in the 13th century it saw plenty of action when the sisters of a Cistercian convent gained a riotous reputation. Under Napoleon an archive of city affairs took over the building.
⊗ *Castello • Map G3*

Calle del Paradiso

9 Calle del Paradiso
Though slightly lop-sided, a delicately sculptured 15th-century arch representing the Virgin and her devotees never fails to delight. The attractive alley is lined with medieval-style timber overhangs.
⊗ *Castello • Map F4*

10 Campo della Maddalena
Unchanged since medieval times, this lovely raised square often doubles as a film set. Its modest houses are topped with chimneys in varying styles.
⊗ *Cannaregio • Map D2*

Top 10 Animals in Venice

1 Pigeons
Piazza San Marco wouldn't be the same without them, but their droppings play havoc with the stonework.

2 Lions
Symbol of Venice and St Mark, abundant statuary and paintings of lions in varying forms fill the city.

3 Cats
The city's feline population is pampered and fed by affectionate Venetians.

4 Rats
Rare, thanks to imported Syrian cats in the past, replaced by an effective council eradication campaign.

5 Horses
Once ridden around town by the Venetian nobility, even up the Campanile via a ramp.

6 Dogs
By law dogs in Venice must be muzzled, kept on a leash and cleaned up after at all times.

7 Seagulls
Self-appointed garbage collectors, they do an admir-able job around the markets.

8 Cormorants
Hundreds of elegant jet-black waterfowl inhabit the lagoon, to the chagrin of the fishermen.

9 Rhinoceroses
One of the many exotic circus animals portrayed on canvas by 18th-century artist Pietro Longhi.

10 Elephants
Incredibly, a runaway elephant from an 1819 circus took refuge in a church, and cannon fire was needed to dispatch it.

Left **Shakespeare** Centre left **Carlo Goldoni** Centre right **Thomas Mann** Right **Ernest Hemingway**

🔟 Writers and Venice

1 Carlo Goldoni

"Italy's Molière" (1707–93) is celebrated at the Venetian theatre named in his honour *(see p66)*. Performances of his lively, witty comedies are staged in Venetian dialect and peopled with recognizable local characters. The prolific playwright moved to Paris and was rewarded with a royal pension, but he died destitute due to the French Revolution.

2 Thomas Mann

The sombre 1912 novel *Death in Venice* was both written and set in Venice and the Lido resort by the German Nobel Prize-winner (1875–1955). It tells the story of an ageing writer in dire need of relaxation who visits the city, but in the wake of an impossible infatuation slowly succumbs to the spreading cholera epidemic and dies.

Johann Wolfgang von Goethe

3 William Shakespeare

Although he never visited Italy, let alone Venice, the English Bard (1564–1616) used accounts by contemporary travellers for the plots of *The Merchant of Venice* and *Othello*, portraying a city buzzing with trade and intrigue. *Romeo and Juliet* is set in Verona *(see p124)*.

4 Thomas Coryate

The very first English-language traveller to write a detailed description of Venice, this eccentric gentleman from Somerset, England (1577–1617) compiled *Crudities, with Observations of Venice* (1611): "Such is the rarenesse of the situation of Venice that it doth even amaze and drive into admiration all strangers that upon their first arrival behold the same."

5 Johann Wolfgang von Goethe

The story goes that this German literary giant (1749–1832) had his first ever view of the sea from Venice's Campanile. Attracted by the lands south of the Alps, his first visit was an experience of personal renewal, the account published as *Italian Journey* (1786–8).

6 Lord Byron

Eccentricities such as a menagerie of foxes and monkeys, not to mention swimming feats in the Grand Canal, made

For more on Shakespeare's Verona See p124

the English Romantic poet (1788–1824) something of a legend during his three-year sojourn here. His Venice-inspired work included *The Two Foscari* and the fourth canto of his autobiographical work *Childe Harold's Pilgrimage*.

John Ruskin

7 John Ruskin
The meticulous if opinionated labour of love of this British art critic (1819–1900), *The Stones of Venice*, was the first work to focus the attention of visitors on the city's unique architectural heritage and Gothic style, as opposed to the art. The book was largely the outcome of an 1849 visit.

8 Henry James
The leitmotif of this US novelist (1843–1916) was the contrast between what he saw as the spontaneity of the New World and the staidness of Europe. Between 1872 and 1909 he compiled *Italian Hours*, a "travel diary" with plenty of comments on Venice.

9 Ernest Hemingway
This US Nobel Prize winner (1899–1961) experienced Italy first-hand as a volunteer ambulance driver during World War I (recounted in *A Farewell to Arms*) and he was wounded near Treviso. *Across the River and into the Trees* is set in Harry's Bar (see p21).

10 Charles Dickens
The great English novelist (1812–70) spent a brief period in Venice during a tour of Italy, and the city inspired a dream sequence in his work *Pictures from Italy* (1846).

Top 10 Background Reads

1 Venice, Jan Morris
An expert account of the delights of the city and its maritime history.

2 Venice, an Anthology Guide, Milton Grundy
A guide around town, seen through the eyes of famous writers.

3 Ruskin's Venice, editor Arnold Whittick
A very readable version of Ruskin's landmark work.

4 Death in Venice, Thomas Mann
A portrayal of desire and decadence amid the fog.

5 Stone Virgin, Barry Unsworth
A mystery involving the 15th-century statue of a famous courtesan.

6 Casanova, or the Art of Happiness, Lydia Flem
An inspired biography of the famous seducer (see p52).

7 Dead Lagoon, Michael Dibdin
Detective Aurelio Zen navigates Venice's murky waters wrought with unease and intrigue.

8 The Architecture of Venice, Deborah Howard
An unbeatable architectural classic.

9 Venice: A Maritime Republic, Frederic C. Lane
A comprehensive history of the city's maritime prowess.

10 Acqua Alta, Donna Leon
From the best-selling mystery series featuring detective Guido Brunetti.

Left **Marco Polo** Centre **Daniele Manin** Right **Giovanni Casanova**

🔟 Outstanding Venetians

1 Marco Polo
Legendary Cathay and the kingdom of the mighty Kublai Khan took pride of place in explorer Marco Polo's best-selling account of his 20-year odyssey to the Far East, *Il milione*. Son of a Venetian merchant, Marco Polo (1254–1324) is responsible for the introduction of pasta and window blinds to the western world.

2 Antonio Vivaldi
Vivaldi (1678–1741) was both an accomplished musician and an influential composer. Of his 500 concertos, *The Four Seasons* is the best known, though 10 were transcribed by J.S. Bach. Vivaldi spent extended periods teaching music at the Pietà home for girls *(see p66)*.

Prolific Venetian composer Antonio Vivaldi

3 Giovanni Casanova
This marvellous romantic figure (1725–98) was variously a diplomat, scholar, trainee priest, adventurer, gambler, notary's clerk, violinist, womanizer, exile, millionaire, writer and spy. Casanova was imprisoned in the Doge's Palace *(see pp12–15)* on charges of being a magician, from where he effected an infamously daring escape.

4 Claudio Monteverdi
This late Renaissance madrigalist (1567–1643) is attributed with the introduction of the solo voice to theatre. His opera *Proserpina Rapita* was the first to be performed in Venice. After long periods at the court of the Gonzagas, he accepted an appointment at the Basilica San Marco and worked for the Scuola Grande di San Rocco *(see p81)*.

5 John Cabot
Italian navigator Giovanni Caboto, or John Cabot (1450–99), and his sons were authorized by Henry VII of England to search for new lands with the aim of furthering trade. Believing himself on the northeast coast of Asia, he discovered Newfoundland in Canada and claimed it for England, opening up cod fishing.

6 Elena Lucrezia Corner Piscopia
It was inconceivable for the church in 1678 that a woman should teach religion, so the University of Padua awarded this child prodigy and the first woman graduate (1646–84) a degree in philosophy, instead of one in theology to which she aspired.

7 Daniele Manin

Organizer of the 1848 rebellion against Austrian rule, the Venetian patriot (1804–57) is commemorated by a statue in Campo Manin. An independent "republic" was declared and survived 17 months of bombardments and even cholera, concluding with Manin's exile to Paris.

8 Paolo Sarpi

When the pope excommunicated Venice for insubordination, involving restrictions on church construction and the refusal to hand over two priests on criminal charges, Sarpi (1552–1623) resolved the rupture. A patriot and theologian, he was an advocate of division between State and Church.

9 Caterina Cornaro

This Venetian noblewoman (1454–1510) married the king of Cyprus then allegedly poisoned him, thus securing the strategic island for Venice. Her return to the city was an occasion of great pomp, recalled to this day in a waterborne procession during the Regata

Queen of Cyprus, Caterina Cornaro

Storica *(see p62)*. Cornaro's reward was the hilltown of Asolo.

10 Luigi Nono

This musician (1924–90) made milestone progress in the field of electronic music, and an archive named after him was set up in Venice in 1993. A committed Communist, his works were often provocative.

Top 10 Foreign Communities

1 Greeks
Since 1498 the longest surviving group, still active with their own church.

2 Armenians
Fleeing Turkish invasion, in 1717 the close-knit religious group was granted an island by the Republic *(see p116)*.

3 Dalmatians (Slavs)
Active traders whose boats gave their name to the Riva degli Schiavoni *(see p101)*.

4 Turks
Sworn political enemies of Venice, the Republic still rented them a trade centre between 1621 and 1898.

5 Jews
The Spanish Inquisition triggered the move here for many Jews expelled from other European countries.

6 Albanians
Calle degli Albanesi near Piazza San Marco is named in honour of this large 15th-century community.

7 Germans
The former German trade headquarters Fondaco dei Tedeschi attracted artists such as Albrecht Dürer.

8 British
Extended sojourns here were mandatory for British upper classes during the 19th-century Grand Tour.

9 French
Impressionist Monet and writers Théophile Gautier and Marcel Proust were attracted to the city in the late 1800s.

10 Americans
Leading literary figures and patrons of the arts have paid long-term visits since the 19th century.

Left **Macello façade** Right **Cantieri Navali research centre**

Historic Conversions

1 Zecca

This elegant waterfront mint was designed by Jacopo Sansovino *(see p45)* and completed in 1545, although a former mint had existed here since 1277. Operations came to a halt in 1870 and in 1905 the building became the home of the Marciana Library. ⊗ *Piazza S Marco, S Marco 4299 • Map Q5 • Closed to the public*

2 Cotonificio

Now occupied by the university architecture faculty, these former cotton mills are a fine example of re-using the city's derelict industrial buildings. The mills and their 1,000 employees were active from 1883 to 1960. ⊗ *Fondamenta Bari, Dorsoduro 864 • Map A5 • Closed to the public*

3 Arsenale

The 300-m (980-ft) long Corderie building in the historic Arsenale shipyards is the perfect setting for the Biennale Arts show held here since 1980 *(see p101)*, but in the past endless lengths of hemp rope were manufactured here. The Gaggiandre docks and 16th-century sailmaking area were adapted into a theatre in 1999 *(see p101)*.

4 Molino Stucky

Plans are afoot to convert this impressive Hanseatic Gothic flour mill dominating the Giudecca Canal into a conference and hotel complex. Built between 1897–1920, workers pale-faced from flour were a common sight until 1954 when operations ceased. ⊗ *Campo S Biagio, Giudecca 810 • Map C*

5 Magazzini del Sale

The lagoon's salt pans largely contributed to the Republic's trade monopoly and salt was stored in these cavernous 14th-century warehouses.The buildings now store boats. ⊗ *Zattere, Dorsoduro 864 • Map C5 • Closed to the public*

Arsenale façade, Castello

6 Deposito del Megio

Few children can boast such a historic home for their primary schooling. A stone lion presides over this former state grain store, essential during the 1559 famine. It was converted in 1921–22. ⊗ *Calle del Megio, S Croce 1179 • Map M1 • Closed to the public*

7 Macello

The Neo-Classical former abattoir, its façade aptly decorated with bucranium (sculpted ox skulls), was restructured by the university when it was granted the premises in 1986. ⊗ *Fondamenta di S Giobbe, Cannaregio 879 • Map B1 • Closed to the public*

Junghans Factory, now apartments

8 Cantieri Navali

A state-of-the-art research centre on coastal and marine technology now accounts for another vast area of the Arsenale. The 16th–19th-century shipyards, set amid a lush garden, were converted in 1991. ⊗ *Arsenale, Castello 2737/F • Map G3 • Closed to the public*

9 CIGA Warehouses

One of the city's best public sports facilities is located in this series of modest repositories, including an indoor swimming pool, gym and bowls facilities. ⊗ *S Alvise, Cannaregio 3190 • Map C1 • Open daily (hours vary) • Admission charge*

10 Junghans Factory

New York-style loft apartments have been created from an old clock factory – one of many conversion projects taking place on Giudecca. ⊗ *Giudecca 801 • Map E6 • Closed to the public*

Left **Cantina Do Mori** Centre **Osteria alla Botte** Right **Al Bottegon**

🔟 Osterie (Wine Bars)

1 Cantina Do Mori
Rows of copper polenta pots hang overhead in this dark, popular bar, billed as the city's oldest *osteria*. The affable owners pour wine directly from huge demijohns and serve delicate postage stamp-sized ham and salad sandwiches *(francobolli)*. 🕲 *Calle dei Do Mori, S Polo 429 • Map N2*

2 Osteria alla Patatina (Al Ponte)
Piping hot wedges of fried potato served on skewers *(patatine)* are the mainstay here, though don't neglect the other tasty morsels, such as delicately battered vegetable strips, to be washed down with some Veneto red or white wines served from bottles or demi-johns. 🕲 *Ponte S Polo, S Polo 2741 • Map M3*

Osteria alla Patatina (Al Ponte)

3 Banco Giro, Osteria da Andrea
A welcome new watering hole in a converted market store at Rialto, where Andrea guarantees quality Italian vintages and tasty nibbles. On the seasonal menu is *carpaccio di tonno alla rucola* (marinated tuna with rocket). 🕲 *Campo S Giacometto, S Polo 122 • Map N2*

4 Osteria del Sacro e Profano
Well worth hunting out near Rialto, this rustic-looking *osteria* is the haunt of international artists who happily mingle with the locals. Wines from the Veneto and Friuli are served with traditional snacks such as *uova con acciughe* (hard-boiled egg with anchovy). 🕲 *Ramo III Parangon, S Polo 502 • Map N2*

5 Osteria Sora al Ponte
A boisterous establishment run by a market family ensures an entertaining visit. Traditional fare such as *bisatei fritti* (fried baby eels) and tripe are worth trying with your carafe of wine. 🕲 *Ponte delle Becarie, S Polo 1588 • Map N2*

6 Osteria alla Frasca
Billed as the site where Titian kept his paints and canvases, this tiny picturesque bar serves drinks and snacks on a vine-covered terrace in summer. 🕲 *Corte della Carità, Cannaregio 5176 • Map D2*

7 Enoteca do Colonne

Animated neighbourhood bar with all manner of counter food ranging from *baccalà* (salted cod) on crusty bread or hearty *musetto* sausage, served with great smiles by Carlo and his jovial daughters. Decent selection of Veneto wines too. ⊗ *Rio Terrà del Cristo, Cannaregio 1814C • Map C2*

8 Osteria alla Botte

You have to fight your way through the locals here, attracted by the lively atmosphere and counter over- flowing with drinkable local wines and appetizing snacks such as fried sardines in breadcrumbs. ⊗ *Calle della Bissa, S Marco 5482 • Map Q3*

Wine cask

9 Trattoria Ca' d'Oro alla Vedova

Young enterprising management has recently taken over this timber-panelled establishment which has been serving mouth-watering counter snacks *(cicheti)* such as crispy battered artichokes and quaffable wine for longer than any of the regulars can remember. ⊗ *Calle del Pistor, Cannaregio 3912 • Map E2*

10 Al Bottegon

Not far from the Accademia Bridge, join the locals at this family-run specialist wine cellar that serves excellent Prosecco at the stand-up bar. Simple nibbles to accompany the wine include *mortadella* sausage and *panini* rolls filled with *sopressa*, a local salami. ⊗ *Fondamenta Nani, Dorsoduro 992 • Map L6*

Top 10 Drinks

1 Spritz
Unrivalled Venetian favourite of white wine with a splash of Bitter, Aperol or Select (apéritif brands) and a shot of mineral water.

2 Prosecco
Excellent naturally sparkling dry white wine from the hills around Conegliano and Valdobbiadene.

3 Bellini
Smooth fresh peach juice and sparkling Prosecco blend, invented by Cipriani of Harry's Bar *(see p21)*.

4 Red Wine
An *ombra* means a small glass of house wine, other-wise try quality Cabernet, Valpolicella or Amarone.

5 White Wine
Soave and Pinot Grigio are worthwhile alternatives to house varieties.

6 Mineral Water
Widely consumed in Italy, either sparkling *(con gas)* or still *(senza gas)*. Tap water is *acqua dal rubinetto*.

7 Fruit Drinks
These can be ordered as *spremuta* (freshly squeezed juice) or *succo di frutta* (bottled nectars).

8 Coffee
Straight *espresso*, frothy *cappuccino* or *caffè latte* in a tall glass with hot milk.

9 Tea
Usually served with a slice of lemon, though herbal tea *(infuso)*, such as camo-mile, is common.

10 After-dinner Sgroppino
A well-kept local secret concocted with lemon sorbet, vodka and Prosecco.

For Venice nightspots **See pp60–61**

Left **Fiaschetteria Toscana** Right **Do Forni**

🔟 Places to Eat in Venice

1 Cipriani
Restaurant guests are ferried over to this hotel-restaurant by the Cipriani's private launch from Piazza San Marco for a memorable gastronomic experience. The fixed-price buffet lunch will set you back a hefty sum, but the setting is wonderful. One house speciality is *tagliolini gratinati al prosciutto* (ribbon pasta with ham, browned in the oven).
◈ Giudecca 10 • Map E6 • 041 520 77 44 • Closed Nov–Mar • €€€€€

2 Da Fiore
Reservations are essential at this sophisticated restaurant, where the owners base the day's menu on what is fresh at the market. With any luck they might have *ravioli di pesce e asparagi* (home-made pasta filled with fish and asparagus), or *moleche fritte con polenta* (fried soft-shelled crab with cornmeal).
◈ Calle del Scaleter, S Polo 2202/A • Map M3 • 041 721 308 • Closed Sun–Mon • No disabled access • €€€€€

3 Grand Canal, Hotel Monaco
Cuisine of a very high standard, including freshly made pasta with shrimp and seafood risotto, accompanied by the best of European wines. In February 2002 this stunning restaurant on a Grand Canal terrace sadly moved indoors for 18 months while renovations are undertaken.
◈ Calle Vallaresso, S Marco 1325 • Map Q6 • 041 520 00 211 • €€€€€

4 Fiaschetteria Toscana
Historic locale with a court-yard and superb food that has earned it a top reputation. *Filetto di rombo con carciofi* (turbot fillet with artichokes) and *tagliolini neri al ragù di astice* (black cuttlefish pasta with lobster) stand out.
◈ Salizzada S Giovanni Grisostomo, Cannaregio 5719 • Map D2 • 041 528 52 81 • Closed Mon L & Tue • €€€

5 Corte Sconta
This former *osteria* is now a trendy restaurant that serves memorable seafood in a pretty "hidden courtyard" *(corte sconta)*. Don't miss *pincia*, the local bread pudding, for dessert. The house wine is also wonderful. Booking ahead is essential. ◈ Calle del Pestrin, Castello 3886 • Map F4 • 041 522 70 24 • Closed Sun–Mon, Jan, mid-Jul–mid-Aug • €€

Grand Canal, Hotel Monaco

6 Do Forni

Right by Piazza San Marco, frequented by business people and politicians. Customers enter an imitation Orient Express dining car to be greeted by displays of glistening seafood. Book ahead. ◈ Calle Specchieri, S Marco 468 • Map Q5 • 041 523 21 48 • No disabled access • €€€€€

7 Vini da Gigio

Tiny restaurant with a great reputation. Soft-spoken owner Gigio prides himself on his Italian and foreign wines to accompany dishes such as masorini anatre alla buranella (duck Burano-style). ◈ Fondamenta S Felice, Cannaregio 3628/a • Map D2 • 041 528 51 40 • Closed Mon • No disabled access • €€

8 L'Incontro

Friendly restaurant specializing in Sardinian meat dishes such as maialino alla sarda suckling pig with maquis herb myrtle). The wine list includes an excellent Tancaferra from Sardinia. ◈ Rio Terrà Canal, Dorsoduro 3062/A • Map K5 • 041 522 24 04 • €€

9 Ai Canottieri

This osteria at the lagoon end of Cannaregio guarantees a soft breeze on summer evenings. Excellent fish dishes include the moscardini alla Torcellana (baby octopus in a spicy tomato sauce). ◈ Fondamenta di S Giobbe, Cannaregio 690 • Map B2 • 041 717 999 • €

10 Trattoria alla Madonna

Traditional restaurant with an inspiring display of fresh seafood. Spaghetti con nero (with cuttlefish ink sauce) and anguilla fritta (fried eel) are mainstays. No bookings, so expect to queue. ◈ Calle della Madonna, S Polo 594 • Map P3 • 041 522 38 24 • Closed Wed, Jan, Aug • No disabled access • €€€

Top 10 What to Eat

1 Carpaccio
Raw beef sliced thin and sprinkled with flakes of Parmesan cheese or rocket (arugula).

2 Sarde in Saor
Fried sardines marinated in a sweet and sour mixture of onions, currants and pine nuts, invented for sailors at sea for lengthy periods.

3 Antipasto di Frutti di Mare
Seafood platter of baby octopus, anchovies, shrimp or whatever else is in season.

4 Prosciutto e Melone
The sweetness of wedges of fresh rock melon is contrasted by the slightly salty cured Parma ham.

5 Risotto di Pesce
Clams, mussels, shrimp and assorted fish in a heavenly creamy rice dish.

6 Pasta con il Nero di Seppia
Usually spaghetti, combined with a rich sauce of tomato and cuttlefish, thoroughly blackened with the ink.

7 Fegato alla Veneziana
Calves' liver Venetian-style cooked slowly with onions and vinegar.

8 Grilled Fish
Such as coda di rospo (monkfish) or pesce spada (swordfish) from the south.

9 Grilled Vegetables
Radicchio (red chicory) in winter, zucchini (courgettes) and melanzane (aubergine/ eggplant) in summer, and roasted peperoni (peppers).

10 Tiramisù
Dessert with a creamy sauce of eggs and mascarpone between layers of sponge drenched in coffee or liqueur.

For a guide to restaurant prices **See pages 79, 85, 93, 99, 105, 113, 119 and 129**

Left **Casanova Music Café** Right **Bacaro Jazz**

🔟 Nightspots

1 Paradiso Perduto
Call it animated or noisy, but live ethnic music, flowing wine, smoky air and simple seafood are all part of the atmosphere of "Lost Paradise". Always full to the (low) rafters, the crowd often spills out onto the canalside where tables are set up in spring and summer. Bands regularly perform from a moored boat.
⬥ *Fondamenta della Misericordia, Cannaregio 2540 • Map D2*

2 Casanova Music Café
The city's only real disco with enough room for dancing occupies a converted cinema. Latin American rhythms feature on Fridays, the only evening with a compulsory first drink, while Saturday means rock and all other music varieties for the 20–50-year-old clientele. ⬥ *Lista di Spagna, Cannaregio 158/a • Map B2*

3 Fiddler's Elbow Irish Pub
Marvellous, lively atmosphere and great Guinness, naturally. You can always count on action here – a concert of

Fiddler's Elbow Irish Pub

Irish music in the cosy square, a maxi screen for football games, while at Carnival and, of course, St Patrick's Day, this is *the* place to be. ⬥ *Campiello dei Testori, Cannaregio 3847 • Map D2*

4 Ai Musicanti
Fancy hearing "O sole mio!" in an evocative Venetian-style set-up? The top-class orchestra and singers will oblige, as well as performing opera highlights by Verdi and Rossini, music by Vivaldi and Mozart, and Italian folk music. The entrance fee is hefty but includes drinks.
⬥ *Campo S Gallo, S Marco 1092 • Map P5*

5 Casinò Municipale, Palazzo Vendramin-Calerg
A magnificent start to an exciting evening – a special ACTV launch from Piazzale Roma transports hopeful clients down the Grand Canal to the landing stage of the beautiful Renaissance palace, alias City Casino, for a glittering night at the tables or the slot machines. It is also a short walk from the San Marcuola ferry stop. ⬥ *Campiello Vendramin, Cannaregio 204 • Map C2*

6 Martini Scala-Club Piano Bar
This chic locale is the only place in Venice where you can enjoy high-quality cuisine and wine until the small hours of the morning, while being entertained by live music in air-conditioned

For Venice wine bars See pp56–7

omfort. No sleeveless tops or horts, for men or women, are lowed. ⊗ *Campo S Fantin, S Marco 980 • Map N5*

asinò Municipale

Bacaro Jazz
7 An enthusiastic multilingual welcome is extended to all isitors in this lively wine bar hat never seems to close. It oasts almost non-stop service, n extended "happy hour" from –7:30pm and a delicious assortnent of Spanish-style *tapas* snack neals to accompany the wine. ⊗ *Salizzada Fontego dei Tedeschi, S Marco 5546 • Map Q3*

Le Bistrot de Venise
8 An eclectic programme of events here never ceases to entertain, from cabaret to poetry readings, live music and art exhibitions. An added bonus is good wine, French specialities including *crêpes*, and even a dish of pasta prepared to a traditional 15th-century recipe. ⊗ *Calle dei Fabbri, S Marco 4685 • Map P4*

Cantina Vecia Carbonera
9 However late in the evening, you can turn up here and count on live music, a good glass of wine and a crusty *crostino* topped with anchovies or cheese. On summer evenings locals row up to the waterside entrance. ⊗ *Ponte Sant'Antonio, Cannaregio 2329 • Map E2*

Piccolo Mondo
10 This tiny club, which is always packed to the rafters, has a wonderful laid-back atmosphere. The entrance is opposite the Accademia cinema. ⊗ *Calle Contarini Corfù, Dorsoduro 1056/A • Map L6*

Left **Carnival costumes** Centre **Vogalonga** Right **Regata Storica**

🔟 Festivals and Events

1 Carnival

An unmissable 10-day extravaganza that takes over the city as a countdown to Lent. The streets mill with costumed and masked local "nobility" or crazily attired visitors. It gets off to a flying start with the *Volo della Colombina* (flight of the dove), when either an acrobat or a cardboard dove is launched from the Campanile in Piazza San Marco, showering on-lookers with confetti. The grand finale is the explosive Mardi Gras.
🔹 *Feb–Mar, concluding on Shrove Tue, 40 days before Easter*

2 Regata Storica

The word regatta originated in Venice so what better place to enjoy the year's most spectacular event? Ornately decorated boats propelled by costumed oarsmen parade down the Grand Canal bearing passengers dressed as historical dignitaries. A series of furiously contested regattas follows. 🔹 *1st Sun in Sep*

3 Vogalonga

A colourful armada of rowing craft from all over the world embarks on a 32-km (20-mile) non-competitive route around the lagoon's scattered islands. The "Long Row" is a great experience for both participants and on-lookers, who line the Canale di Cannaregio towards midday to cheer on the breathtaking final stretch down the Grand Canal.
🔹 *May: Sun after Ascension*

4 Festa del Redentore

People crowd on to all available watercraft, decorated with paper lanterns and greenery, for a feast of roast duck and watermelon, followed by a midnight fireworks display. It all takes place near Palladio's church on Giudecca *(see p45)* to commemorate the end of the 1576 plague. For those on foot, a temporary pontoon bridge stretches from the Zattere over the Giudecca canal. 🔹 *Mid-Jul: Sat*

5 Biennale Art Exhibition

The world's leading international art bonanza is held on a two-yearly basis. The leafy gardens in eastern Castello are the principal venue, supplemented by the Corderie building in the Arsenale *(see p54)*. 🔹 *Jun–Nov*

Venice Marathon

Madonna della Salute
6 Venetians make a pilgrimage to Longhena's church on the Grand Canal *(see p38)* every winter, to give thanks for the end of the 1630 plague. The area assumes a festive atmosphere with stalls selling candy floss and balloons. ✿ *21 Nov*

Venice Marathon
7 One of the world's most beautiful marathon routes. Runners from all parts of the globe begin this classic 42-km (26-mile) race at Villa Pisani on the Brenta waterway, cross the causeway to Venice, the Zattere and San Marco, and finish near the public gardens in Castello. ✿ *Late Oct*

Su e Zo per i Ponti
8 Anyone can take part in this leisurely non-competitive walk or run "up and down the bridges". A variety of official routes can be followed, and all participants receive a medal on finishing.
✿ *Late Mar/Apr: 4th Sun in Lent*

La Sensa
9 Head for the Riviera di San Nicolò at the Lido *(see p115)* to watch this ancient ceremony of Venice wedding the Sea". A costumed "doge" casts a ring into the sea amid a procession of celebratory boats. Symbolizing Venice's maritime supremacy, the Sensa has been staged since Venice took Istria and Dalmatia in AD 997. ✿ *May: Ascension Day*

Festa di San Rocco
10 The feast day of St Roch, the French saint adopted by the confraternity for alleviating the 576–7 plague, is celebrated each year at the Scuola Grande di San Rocco *(see p81)*. A mass and evening concert conclude the festivities. ✿ *16 Aug*

Top 10 Sports in Venice

Rowing
1 Immensely popular Venetian pastime practised standing-up. Join the oldest club Canottieri Bucintoro.
✿ *Zattere, Dorsoduro • Map C5*

Cycling
2 Illegal in Venice itself though you'll see kids zooming around. Rent a bike on the Lido from Bruno Lazzari.
✿ *Gran Viale 21/B • Map H2*

Sailing
3 Yachtsmen gather at the marina on San Giorgio Maggiore island.

Swimming
4 Head for the Lido, or the crowded indoor pools at Sacca Fisola and Sant'Alvise.
✿ *Map C1*

In-line Skating
5 There is a small rink at Sant'Elena in Castello, otherwise stick to the Lido pavements *(see p115)*.

Golf
6 The well-reputed 18-hole course at the Alberoni is on the south of the Lido.
✿ *Map H2*

Tennis
7 The Lido has the only courts available to visitors.
✿ *Lungomare G Marconi 41/d • Map H2*

Jogging
8 The city's stone paving doesn't do wonders for your knees, so try the city parks.

Gyms
9 Private gyms with state-of-the-art equipment can be found in the *Yellow Pages*.

Football
10 The home team Venezia plays at Sant'Elena stadium on Sundays. ✿ *Map H2*

Left **Spizzico and Burger King** Centre **Feeding the pigeons in San Marco** Right **Ferry trip**

🔟 Places for Children

1 Play Areas

Children tired of art and architecture can release their energy at well-equipped playgrounds with slides, swings and frames at Parco Savorgnan near Ponte delle Guglie in Cannaregio and the fenced-in waterfront park at Giardini in Castello *(see p102)*. The vast shady green expanse of Sant'Elena even boasts a modest skating rink and an artificial climbing wall. Otherwise make friends with the city kids as they kick footballs or cycle around Campo San Polo *(see p81)* of an afternoon.

2 Ferry Trips

Restful for adults, exciting for youngsters, the varied boat lines are an ideal way for families to appreciate the joys of the city. Get older children to plan trips on the route maps but avoid the outside seating on the *vaporetto* with toddlers. For an extended trip, take the majestic double-decker *motonave* over to Lido and Punta Sabbioni *(see p135)*.

Glassmaking demonstration in Murano

3 Doge's Palace Prisons and Armoury

Children are thrilled by the spooky labyrinth of narrow passageways through the palace's erstwhile prisons, and it's fun deciphering the graffiti scratched on the walls by inmates over the centuries. In the armoury, hunt out the unusual child-sized suit from the 16th century, along with the protection for horses *(see pp12–15)*.

4 Museo Storico Navale

Easily the best city museum for children, this three-floor haven of shipbuilding includes Chinese junks and exhibits from World War II, such as the famed torpedoes guided by Italian Navy divers, responsible for sinking British warships *(see p41)*.

5 Museo di Storia Naturale

The star of the marvellous Natural History Museum is a 3.6-m (12-ft) tall and 7-m (23-ft) long skeleton of the dinosaur *Ouranosauris nigeriensis*, discovered in the Sahara Desert by modern-day Venetian explorer Giancarlo Ligabue. Don't miss the Japanese crabs whose claws open to the length of a man's arm
Ⓢ *Salizzada del Fondaco dei Turchi, S Croce 1730 • Map L1 • Closed for restructuring*

6 Glassmaking Demonstrations

Magic moments are guaranteed as children are transfixed by skilful craftsmen blowing blobs molten glass into fine vases, moulding coloured rods into myriad animal shapes. Small workshops are dotted all over Venice, while Murano has more large-scale furnaces – demonstrations are free, on the condition you stroll through the showroom afterwards *(see p109)*.

7 Spizzico and Burger King

A new and welcome introduction to Venice for families, for its indoor children's playground. This centrally located Italian-run hybrid hamburger, pizza and salad outlet has very reasonable prices and plentiful seating. ◎ *Campo S Luca, S Marco 4476 • Map 4 • 041 240 16 05*

8 Feeding the Pigeons

Scattering feed to the birds in Piazza San Marco *(see pp16–19)* while Mum and Dad immortalize you on video is a must for young visitors. Bags of corn are hawked by sellers, but the birds eat anything.

9 Laboratorio Blu Bookshop

Just off the main Cannaregio canal is this delightful bookshop dedicated to youngsters. One stand is packed with illustrated children's books in English, audio cassettes and games. Kids love crawling into the cubby hole to enjoy their purchases. ◎ *Ghetto Vecchio, Cannaregio 1224 • Map C1 • 041 715 819*

10 The Disney Store

Youngsters are greeted by Mickey Mouse on a bridge, while Donald Duck fishes an old boot out of a canal. Usual Disney fare is on sale. ◎ *Campo S Bartolomeo, S Marco 5257/98 • Map P3*

The Disney Store

Left **La Fenice plaque** Centre **Malibran Theatre** Right **Goldoni Theatre**

🔟 Entertainment Venues

1 La Fenice
World-famous opera and concert performances are now held at the Palafenice on Tronchetto, while reconstruction proceeds on the burnt-down opera house *(see p73)*. Productions range from Verdi and Rossini to contemporary composers. Take boat No. 82 or shuttle buses from Piazzale Roma and Mestre. 🚤 *Ticket office: c/o Cassa di Risparmio, Campo S Luca, S Marco 1965 • Map P4 • 041 521 01 61*

2 Teatro Malibran
In a quiet square near Rialto stands the gleaming Malibran Theatre, re-inaugurated in 2001 to take on part of the Fenice's productions. Dating back to 1678 as Teatro Grimani, it was renamed after the 19th-century Spanish mezzo-soprano Maria Malibran. 🚤 *Corte del Teatro Malibran, Cannaregio • Map E3 • 041 521 01 61*

3 Films in English
The Giorgione cinema has English-language screenings one evening a week in winter. In late

Venice Film Festival

summer, the outdoor cinema in Campo San Polo means delights from the Venice Film Festival. 🚤 *Cinema Giorgione: Rio Terrà dei Franceschi, Cannaregio 4612 • Map C2 • 041 522 62 98 • Venice Film Festival: 041 521 87 11 • www.labiennale.org*

4 Teatro Goldoni
One of the oldest theatres in the city, dating from the 17th century. It acquired its present name in 1875 in honour of the 18th-century playwright Carlo Goldoni *(see p50)*. An excellent range of international plays is performed in Italian. 🚤 *Calle del Teatro, S Marco 4650/B • Map P5 • 041 240 20 11*

5 Vivaldi Concerts
A performance of Vivaldi's music in the church where the maestro taught is a moving experience, and overhead are Tiepolo's brilliant ceiling frescoes *(see p101)*. Tickets are available at agencies, hotels or directly at the church. 🚤 *Santa Maria della Pietà, Riva degli Schiavoni, Castello • Map F4 • 041 523 10 96 • www.vivaldi.it*

6 Chamber Music
While you're sighing with the uplifting notes of Vivaldi, Bach or Benedetto Marcello at one of these concerts, take time to appreciate the 80 ancient musical instruments which hang from the walls of the Church of San Bartolomeo *(see p74)*. 🚤 *Calle dei Bombaseri, S Marco 5096 • Map P3 • 041 277 05 61*

7 Concerts in Costume
The youthful Orchestra di Venezia stages tourist-orientated concerts of Boccherini and Albinoni with singers and dancers in authentic 1700s costumes.
◎ *Campiello della Scuola, S Polo 2454* • *Map M3* • *041 522 81 25*

8 Jazz at "900"
Top-quality live jazz music is guaranteed every Wednesday at 9:30pm in this cosy club-pizzeria, with an excellent wine list.
◎ *Novecento (900), Campiello del Sansoni, S Polo 900* • *Map M3* • *041 522 65 65*

"900" jazz club

9 Auditorium Santa Margherita
This converted cinema regularly stages live ethnic and other music, free of charge. The day's programme is generally posted on the door. ◎ *Campo S Margherita, Dorsoduro 3689* • *Map K5* • *041 521 27 65*

10 Teatro Fondamente Nuove
Formerly a lumber store, since 1993 the premises have been buzzing with experimental theatre and contemporary dance. Festivals of off-beat films are also on the avant garde programme.
◎ *Fondamente Nuove, Cannaregio 5013* • *Map E2* • *041 522 44 98*

Top 10 Films set in Venice

1 Indiana Jones and the Last Crusade (1989)
Hero Harrison Ford heaves up the floor in the church of San Barnaba.

2 Moonraker (1979)
Roger Moore as James Bond steers a gondola-cum-hovercraft across Piazza San Marco in a thrilling chase.

3 Death in Venice (1971)
Visconti's film starring Dirk Bogarde is now as classic as the Thomas Mann novel on which it is based *(see p51)*.

4 Don't Look Now (1973)
This thriller, with Donald Sutherland and Julie Christie, will keep you awake at night.

5 The Comfort of Strangers (1990)
Directed by Paul Schrader, this is based on Ian McEwan's enigmatic novel.

6 Eve (1962)
Joseph Losey's black-and-white classic starring "temptress" Jeanne Moreau.

7 Senso (1954)
Alida Valli betrays family and country for an Austrian officer in another Visconti film.

8 Fellini's Casanova (1976)
Donald Sutherland walks around a fantasized version of Venice in this Fellini film.

9 Everyone Says I Love You (1996)
Woody Allen literally runs in to Julia Roberts as they both jog through the city.

10 The Wings of a Dove (1997)
Helena Bonham Carter stars in the film version of Henry James' Venetian story.

Left **Jesurum** Centre **Venini** Right **Rubelli**

🔟 Shops in Venice

1 Mondonovo
Venice's most original *papier-mâché* masks. A monstrous bear's head might hang alongside a gloating Tutankhamun, but the speciality is Carnival costumes. Masks for the film *Eyes Wide Shut* (2000) were made here. ◈ *Rio Terrà Canal, Dorsoduro 3063 • Map D5*

2 Nardi
Elizabeth Taylor, Grace Kelly and Elton John have all happily spent time (and more) in this plush boutique of glittering marvels. Three generations of craftsmen have thrilled those who can afford it with breathtaking pieces, such as their blackamoor brooch in ruby and gold or diamond and platinum. ◈ *Piazza S Marco 69, S Marco • Map Q5*

3 Jesurum
A triumphant showroom of exquisite lace and embroidery, founded in 1870. Ask to see the "back-up copy" of the delicate lace tablecloth commissioned by Queen Margherita which took 10 years to complete. The firm first acted as a trade school for poor girls. ◈ *Piazza S Marco 60–1, S Marco • Map Q5*

4 Venini
Don't expect Venetian glass animals here, rather innovative platters and vases of great simplicity and style. Since its 1921 beginnings, Venini's award-winning design team has included top names Carlo Scarpa and Gae Aulenti. ◈ *Piazzetta Leoncini, S Marco 314 • Map Q4*

5 Perle e Dintorni
String together your own necklace in this great shop. Dazzling kaleidoscopic baubles range from traditional gay murrhine, to blown globes sprayed with gold and silver, Chinese ceramics and African bone beads. ◈ *Calle della Mandola, S Marco 3740 • Map N4*

Traditional Venetian masks on display in Mondonovo

For more on shopping in Venice **See p138**

6 Rizzo

Feel like jet-black tagliatelle ribbons made from cuttlefish ink for dinner? Or perhaps the blue Curaçao variety or the multi-coloured Carnival masks? These are only a taste of more than 40 imaginative pasta shapes by Rizzo – a marvellous souvenir.

Ⓢ Salizzada S Giovanni Grisostomo, Cannaregio 5778 • Map Q2

7 Coin Department Store

It's impossible to walk past the stylishly dressed windows of Coin without being impressed. Centrally located close to the Rialto GPO, this branch of Italy's largest department chain has an elegant clothing range and sleekly designed homeware.

Ⓢ Salizzada S Giovanni Gristomo, Cannaregio 5785 • Map Q2

8 Rubelli

Venice's past contact with the Orient is conjured up by the sumptuous handmade furnish-ings in this showroom. A blend of computer technology and traditional techniques is used for the brocades, damasks and silks.

Ⓢ Campo S Gallo, S Marco 1089 • Map P5

9 Paolo Olbi

Photo albums and address books in rainbow-coloured marbled paper and leather at reasonable prices, by one of the original craftsmen in Venice.

Ⓢ Calle della Mandola, S Marco 3653 • Map N4

10 Venice Pavilion Bookshop

Excellent multilingual selec-tion of literature and miscellany focusing on Venice. Also serves as a tourist information point and box office for cultural events.

Ⓢ Palazzetto Selva, Giardinetti Reali, S Marco 2 • Map Q5

Top 10 Souvenirs

1 Glassware
Impress your guests back home with a genuine Murano chandelier or perhaps a *millefiori* paperweight.

2 Gourmet Food
For something authentically Italian but intrinsically Venetian, try extra virgin olive oil flavoured with chilli peppers, bottled red chicory paste or pasta in the shape of gondolas and masks.

3 T-shirts
The essential guaranteed souvenir of Venice, sold at the ubiquitous street stalls.

4 Masks
A mind-boggling array of masks, traditionally made for Carnival in *papier-mâché*, ceramic and even leather.

5 Marbled Paper
Swirls of pastel hues can be used for covering books or simply as elegant wrapping paper for gifts.

6 Beads
All manner of beads, from frosted glass, ceramic or the traditional colourful murrhine mosaic-style, can be found.

7 Italian Wine and Liqueurs
Take advantage of lower prices and taxes by stocking up on locally produced wines.

8 Fabric
Lace is the most Venetian of materials, but attractive linens and velvets are also good value.

9 Silverwork
Photo frames, letter openers and teaspoons make lovely gifts for friends.

10 Clothes
All the top fashion names can be found in Venice.

AROUND TOWN

VENICE'S TOP 10

Left **Busy streetlife in Campo San Bartolomeo** Right **Designer shopping on Mercerie**

San Marco

VENICE'S SMALLEST BUT FOREMOST sestiere *(district)* named after the city's patron saint is bounded by the Grand Canal on all but one side, which explains the number of stately palaces in the area. It revolves around the buzz of Piazza San Marco and the majestic Doge's Palace, the political and legal core of the city until the 18th century. Running off the square are the Mercerie and Calle Larga XXII Marzo, offering wall-to-wall designer shopping. But beyond that San Marco has a residential air, with a great range of places to eat. Don't hesitate to wander down minor alleyways: surprises include unusual wellheads and many craft workshops.

Sights

1. Piazza San Marco
2. Mercerie
3. Campo San Stefano
4. Teatro La Fenice
5. Scala Contarini del Bovolo
6. Campo San Bartolomeo
7. Chiesa di San Moisè
8. Palazzo Grassi
9. Museo Fortuny
10. Chiesa di Santa Maria del Giglio

Shop on the Mercerie

1 Piazza San Marco
See pp16–19.

2 Mercerie
The expensive elegance of Venice is most evident on this main thoroughfare linking Rialto and Piazza San Marco. *Mercerie* means haberdasher's, although these days it is the realm of the designer fashion outlets who are able to afford the sky-high rents. Just below the ornate Torre dell' Orologio archway is a sculpted female figure commemorating a housewife who lived here rent-free as a reward for inadvertently knocking a mortar into the street, killing a revolutionary leader and thus halting the short-lived Baiamonte Tiepolo revolt in 1310.
● *Map Q4*

3 Campo San Stefano
This spacious, elegant square is edged by cafés with smart, white-jacketed waiters and colourful awnings. Its most regular inhabitants seem to be unhurried pigeons, pecking around the ornate lampposts, and local children at play watched over by nannies and doting grandparents. Pride of place in the centre goes to a statue of Niccolò Tommaseo, patriot and author of the *Risorgimento*. At Carnival time a lively outdoor craft market is held here, although it is not quite up to the level of merry-making seen here in olden times when there were magnifi-cent balls and bull-ghts. The latter events ended in 1802 when a stand collap-sed on spectators.
● *Map M5*

4 Teatro La Fenice
Masked in scaffolding since 1996 when an arson attack left it gutted, the historic "Phoenix" theatre is taking its time rising from the flames, due to legal wrangles. Selva's 1792 opera house, just one of 17 theatres at the time, has staged countless world premieres including Rossini's *Tancredi* in 1813, five operas commissioned of Verdi, most notably *Rigoletto* and *La Traviata*, and more recent works by Stravinsky and Luigi Nono. Legendary divas Maria Callas and Dame Joan Sutherland have sung in this glorious setting.
● *Campo S Fantin* • *Map N5*

5 Scala Contarini del Bovolo
Often used as a film set, this fine 15th-century palace with its beautiful external "snail-shell" staircase is squeezed into a diminutive square. Following careful restoration, visitors can now climb the winding steps via five floors of loggias to a dome sheltering a splendid belvedere. From here there are magical views over the city's rooftops.
● *Corte dei Risi, S Marco 4299* • *Map P4*
• *Open Apr–Oct: 10am–6pm daily;*
Nov–Mar: 10am–4pm Sat–Sun
• *Admission charge*

Antiques shop, Campo San Stefano

Glassmaking

Venetian glasswork exquisitely decorates chandeliers, chalices and mirrors and has long been in demand the world over, especially during the Golden Age of the 16th century. Although the industry moved to Murano in 1295 as a safety measure against fire decreed by the Great Council, many furnaces around the San Marco district welcome visitors.

6 Campo San Bartolomeo

The statue of celebrated Venetian playwright Carlo Goldoni scrutinizes the milling crowds on this crossroads square. Strategically placed for a host of inviting bars crammed into the alleys radiating off it, "San Bartolo" serves as the main hang-out for the city's young and trendy. The northern end is occupied by the main post office, once home to Venice's German community *(see p53)*. They worshipped in the Chiesa di San Bartolomeo, since deconsecrated and now a venue for chamber music concerts. Ⓢ *Map P3*

7 Chiesa di San Moisè

So overloaded was the 1668 façade of this church with ostentatious Baroque stone decorations that several statues were removed in 1878 to save it from collapse. It has been blasted by critics as "the height of architectural folly" and by John Ruskin *(see p51)* as "one of the basest examples of the basest school of the Renaissance". Devoid of religious symbols, it is given over wholly to the glorification of the aristocratic Fini family, who laid out 30,000 ducats for the job. Ⓢ *Campo S Moisè, S Marco 4299 • Map P5 • Open 3:30–6:30pm daily • Free*

8 Palazzo Grassi

As of 1985, the splendid salons of Fiat's Palazzo Grassi, superbly restored under the supervision of leading architect Gae Aulenti, have been the setting for numerous high-profile exhibitions focusing on major archaeological or art themes, such as the Etruscans, Phoenicians and Futurists. Set on the Grand Canal, the palace itself dates back to 1740 when a wealthy merchant family commissioned Giorgio Massari to design the building. Entrance is via the picturesque tree-shaded Campo San Samuele, which features a graceful Veneto-Byzantine bell tower. Ⓢ *S Samuele, S Marco 3231 • Map L5 • Open for exhibitions • Admission charge*

9 Museo Fortuny

Flamboyant Spanish artist and theatrical stage designer Mariano Fortuny y Madrazo (1871–1950) adopted Venice as his home and muse, and transformed this ponderous 15th-century palace in Gothic-Venetian style into an

Palazzo Grassi façade

Chiesa di Santa Maria del Giglio

exotic atelier. Although restoration is on-going, a number of rooms are open for temporary exhibitions. In the near future visitors will be able to admire Fortuny's sumptuous velvets, renowned the world over, his famous pleated silk dresses, lamps, paintings, a remarkable stage curtain and fascinating 19th-century photographs.
Ⓢ Campo S Beneto, S Marco 3780 • Map N4 • Open for exhibitions • Admission charge

10 Chiesa di Santa Maria del Giglio

Opening on to a lovely square next to the Grand Canal, this church is a further example of Venetian Baroque extravagance. Commissioned by the Barbaro family, its façade exalts their generations of maritime and political triumphs, with crests, galleys and statues. Relief maps along the lower plinth depict Zara, Candia, Padua, Rome, Corfu and Spalato, the fortified cities where many family members had served. Ⓢ Campo S Maria del Giglio, S Marco 3231 • Map N6 • Open 10am–5pm Mon– Sat, 1–5pm Sun • Admission charge

A Day in San Marco

Morning

🕐 Visit the **Doge's Palace** on Piazza San Marco first (see pp12–15), arriving early to fit it all in. Must-sees are the Sala del Senato, Sala del Maggior Consiglio, prisons and the Bridge of Sighs. Then take a break for coffee in the modern café in the palace's former stables and watch the gondolas glide past the glassed-in doorway.

Time your visit to **Basilica San Marco** (see pp8–11) for midday, to catch the mosaics illuminated by huge spotlights so they glitter to their utmost. The tiles were laid at angles to catch the light.

🍴 Lunch at **Harry's Bar**, as Hemingway's hero did in Across the River and into the Trees. Order the carpaccio, wafer thin slices of raw beef, invented here by Cipriani (see p21).

Afternoon

🛍 The **Mercerie** (see p73) is shopper's heaven, packed with international high fashion stores from Benetton to Cartier, and classy souvenir glass and hand-crafted paper workshops. For yet more, cross over to Calle Larga XXII Marzo for designer delights such as **Bulgari** jewellery and **Frette** linens (see p76).

Return to **Piazza San Marco** (see pp16–19) in time to enjoy the views over Venice and the lagoon from the Campanile at dusk. At ground level again, it's time for a Bellini apéritif at **Caffè Florian** (see p17) to watch the sun set over the façade of the basilica.

Left **Frette** Centre **Benetton** Right **Cartier**

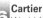 Designer Boutiques

1 Frette
Since 1860 Frette has been importing top-grade cotton from Egypt and transforming it into towels and custom-made household linen. ◈ *Calle Larga XXII Marzo, S Marco 2070/A • Map Q4*

2 L'Isola – Carlo Moretti
Contemporary glass at its innovative best, exhibited in galleries all over the world. Moretti's trademarks are "paper cone" vases, tumblers and huge sculptures. ◈ *Campo S Moisè, S Marco 1468 • Map P5*

3 Marforio
Easy to find, with its well-known coloured glass umbrellas near Rialto, this store is a great favourite for its extensive range of brand-name wallets, elegant handbags and travel accessories. ◈ *Campo S Salvador, S Marco 5033 • Map P3*

4 Benetton
The vibrant colours and simple styles of T-shirts, jackets and jeans attract buyers young and old to the two-floor premises close to Piazza San Marco. Shoes and bags are recent additions. ◈ *Mercerie, S Marco 712 • Map Q4*

5 Epicentro
Alessi kettles, heart-shaped hot-water bottles, designer garlic presses – you'll find the perfect gift here for friends who think they have everything. ◈ *Calle dei Fabbri, S Marco 932 • Map P4*

6 Cartier
World-famous French jewellers whose fortress-like premises gleam with gold, precious stones, handbags and watches. ◈ *Mercerie S Zulian, S Marco 606 • Map Q4*

7 MaxMara
For more than 50 years this family company has been designing fashionable clothes and accessories for city girls. ◈ *Mercerie, S Marco 268–70 • Map Q4*

8 Bulgari
Striking contemporary jewellery, watches, accessories and Rosenthal porcelain. ◈ *Calle Larga XXII Marzo, S Marco 2282 • Map Q4*

9 Fratelli Rossetti
Superb Italian elegance from this 50-year-old family-run firm, known worldwide for shoes, belts, bags and jackets. ◈ *Campo S Salvador, S Marco 4800 • Map P3*

10 Fendi
Flamboyant frocks and shoes for special occasions and crazily beaded bags, all with the "double-F" Fendi mark. ◈ *S Moisè, S Marco 1474 • Map P5*

For more on shopping in Venice **See p138**

eft **Leon d'Oro** Centre **Legatoria Piazzesi** Right **Bevilacqua**

10 Craft Shops

1 Venetia Studium
Exquisite hanging silk lamps f Fortuny design are reproduced vith hand-painted patterning and lass beading. ◊ *Calle Larga XXII Marzo, S Marco 2403–6 • Map Q4*

2 Legatoria Piazzesi
The only people in Venice till printing paper with hand-cut locks, as well as binding books. ◊ *Campiello della Feltrina, S Marco 2511 Map P6*

3 Pagnacco
Polar bears, squirrels and angaroos are but some of the 00 glass animals this wonderful hop boasts. Orchestras of tiny lass musicians fill the shop vindow. ◊ *Mercerie, S Marco 231 Map Q4*

4 Leon d'Oro
Commedia dell'arte marion-ttes, musical puppet theatres nd glittering carnival masks for ale or hire. ◊ *Frezzeria, S Marco 770 • Map P5*

5 Galleria Livio De Marchi
Crumpled boots and a rain-oat slung over a chair are actu-lly sculptures – there are even fe-size wooden cars, complete vith engines. ◊ *Salizzada S Samuele, Marco 3157/A • Map L5*

6 Rigattieri
Ceramic enthusiasts must ot miss this extraordinary shop f beautiful pottery. ◊ *Calle dei rati, S Marco 3535/36 • Map M5*

7 Valese Fonditore
The Valese family foundry has been creating animals, lamps and door knockers in brass and bronze since 1913. Examples of their work can be found in Buckingham Palace and The White House. ◊ *Calle Fiubera, S Marco 793 • Map Q4*

8 Bevilacqua
Weaving looms from the 1700s are still used to produce velvet and silk cushions, tapes-tries and curtain tassels. ◊ *Campo S Moisè, S Marco 2520 • Map P5*

9 Bottega del Mondo
A kaleidoscopic display of handwoven shawls from India and musical instruments from Cameroon are part of an enterprise to guarantee artisans a just income. ◊ *Salizzada Pio X, S Marco 5164 • Map P3*

10 Rolando Segalin
As well as the brocade slippers and bizarre footwear with built-in toes, this long-established cobbler also makes special order shoes. ◊ *Calle dei Fuseri, S Marco 4365 • Map P4*

Left **Devil's Forest Pub** Centre **Bar al Teatro** Right **Le Café**

Bars and Cafés

1 Pasticceria Rosa Salva
The coffee and cake shop for Venetians. The narrow bar only does counter service, so you have to stand up for your *cappuccino* and croissant for breakfast or Campari soda in the evening. Delectable ice cream in summer. ⊙ *Campo S Luca, S Marco 4589 • Map P4*

2 Pasticceria Marchini
No drinks or seating, but a paradise for those with a sweet tooth. Orange and pistachio chocolates come in Venetian mask shapes. ⊙ *Ponte S Maurizio, S Marco 2769 • Map N6*

3 Caffè Brasilia
Tuck in to a huge fresh fruit salad smothered with yogurt or a *tramezzino* sandwich in this quiet side-alley café. The coffee's good too. ⊙ *Calle dei Assassini, S Marco 3658 • Map N4*

4 Bar al Teatro
Pretty trellising in the lovely patio cleverly hides the scaffolding around the Fenice Theatre next door *(see p73)*. Lean on the bar to munch a toasted sandwich. ⊙ *Campo S Fantin, S Marco 1916 • Map N5*

5 Devil's Forest Pub
This "pub" sports a real red London phonebox, draught beers and ales, light meals served until midnight and even a dartboard and live music. ⊙ *Calle dei Stagneri, S Marco 5185 • Map Q3*

6 Inguanotto
Venetian sweetmeats can be enjoyed here, but most come for the Spritz apéritif, reputedly the best in town *(see p57)*. ⊙ *Ponte dell'Ovo, S Marco 4819 • Map P4*

7 Le Café
Have a fresh orange juice or a *cappuccino* and pastry as you watch life go by in the square. ⊙ *Campo S Stefano, S Marco 2797 • Map M5*

8 Osteria ai Do Ladroni
A friendly place for a drink and tasty bar snack such as meat-filled breadcrumbed olives. ⊙ *Ramo del Fontego dei Tedeschi, S Marco 5362 • Map P3*

9 McDonald's
Burgers and French fries at approachable prices, though the decor is the same the world over ⊙ *Calle Larga S Marco 656 • Map Q4*

10 Ai Assassini
A great *osteria* in a cul-de-sac near the Fenice. Stand at the bar for appetizing snacks or treat yourself to a table. ⊙ *Rio Terrà dei Assassini, S Marco 3695 • Map N4*

For more Venice wine bars **See pp56–7**

Price Categories

For a three-course meal for one with half a bottle of wine (or equivalent meal), taxes and extra charges

€	under €30
€€	€30–€40
€€€	€40–€50
€€€€	€50–€60
€€€€€	over €60

Left **Ristorante all'Angelo** Right **Rosticceria San Bartolomeo**

10 Places to Eat

1 Hostaria à Masaniello
Marvellous southern Italian eatery. The menu includes buffalo mozzarella shipped daily from Naples. ✆ Campo S Stefano, S Marco 2801 • Map M5 • 041 520 90 03 • €€

2 Ristorante alla Borsa
A great selection of wines accompany dishes such as cernia al cartoccio (sea bass with clams, mussels, tomatoes and capers). ✆ Calle delle Veste, S Marco 2018 • Map P6 • 041 523 54 34 • €€

3 Ristorante all'Angelo
A long-running favourite with seating for 700. Try the risotto di seppie (rice cooked with cuttlefish black ink sauce). ✆ Calle Larga S Marco, S Marco 403 • Map Q4 • 041 520 92 99 • €

4 Rosticceria San Bartolomeo
Try the local favourite here, mozzarella in carozza, a deep-fried cheese sandwich. ✆ Calle della Bissa, S Marco 5423 • Map N5 • 041 522 35 69 • No disabled access • €

5 Chat qui rit
Self-service restaurant with generous plates of pasta and salads served inside or out. ✆ Calle Tron, S Marco 1131 • Map P5 • 041 522 90 86 • No credit cards • €

6 Leon Bianco
Great for a cheap lunch of pasta e fagioli (bean and pasta soup) or lasagne, at the bar or at a table out the back. ✆ Campo S Luca, S Marco 4153 • Map P4 • 041 522 11 80 • No credit cards • €

7 Al Bacareto
A 30-year institution. Try the bigoli in salsa (spaghetti with anchovy and onion purée). Non-smoking rooms and outdoor seating too. ✆ Calle delle Botteghe, S Marco 3447 • Map M5 • 041 528 93 36 • €€

8 Al Vaporetto
Spacious self-service eatery. Choice of hot meals, pizza or rolls. ✆ Calle della Mandola, S Marco 3726 • Map N4 • 041 522 94 98 • €

9 La Caravella
Resembling a caravel sailing ship, the trestle tables are adorned with pewter plates. Fish and meat dishes and good wine list. ✆ Via XXII Marzo, S Marco 2398 • Map P5 • 041 520 89 01 • €€€€€

10 Acqua Pazza
Owner Antonio from Amalfi serves Mediterranean cuisine, including Neapolitan-style pizza. ✆ Campo Sant'Angelo, S Marco 3808/10 • Map N5 • 041 277 06 88 • €€€

Note: Unless otherwise stated, all restaurants accept credit cards and serve vegetarian meals

Left **Scuola Grande di San Rocco** Right **Campo San Giacomo dell'Orio**

San Polo and Santa Croc

VENICE'S GREATEST CONCENTRATION *of sights can be found in these neighbouring districts, a the geographical heart of Venice, having grown up around the ancient core of Rialto where the first inhabitants settled. Here, glorious churches, landmark monuments and breathtaking palaces are all saturated in history. Essential sights include Santa Maria Gloriosa dei Frari, the Scuola Grande di San Rocco where Tintoretto demonstrated his genius on sumptuous canvases, and the morning bustle of Rialto market. The squares of San Polo and San Giacomo dell'Orio are both full of cafés and benches for resting weary feet.*

🔟 Sights

1 Rialto Market
2 Campo San Polo
3 Scuola Grande di San Rocco
4 Campo San Giacomo dell'Orio
5 Chiesa di San Giacomo dell'Orio
6 Scuola Grande di San Giovanni Evangelista
7 Palazzo Mocenigo
8 Giardino Papadopoli
9 Campo San Zan Degolà
10 Ca' Pesaro Museo de Arte Orientale

Interior detail, Scuola Grand di San Rocco

Rialto Market

See pp28–9.

Campo San Polo

This lovely square undergoes series of transformations, from tractive theatre or dance area uring Carnival, to open-air nema through the summer nonths, and playground for icycle- and scooter-mad kids the est of the year. It has never een particularly quiet – it was nce a venue for bullfights and ird-netting, extravagant parties vith fireworks displays and even rime. In 1548 Florentine writer n hiding Lorenzino de' Medici vas stabbed to death here on rders from the great Cosimo e' Medici. It was punishment or the assassination of Cosimo's ousin Duke Alessandro, which rought the Medici line to an nd. ✪ *Map M3*

Scuola Grande di San Rocco

linding in the morning sun hanks to its cleansing face-lift, he early Renaissance façade of his historic building, home to nasterpieces by Tintoretto, is a

açade of Scuola Grande di San Rocco

marvel of intertwined sculpted stone wreaths and crouching elephants dwarfed by admirable columns. The Istrian stone facing is embedded with a rainbow medley of burgundy porphyry and green and cream veined marble inserts. Designed by Bartolomeo Bon in 1517 and successively added to by Scarpagnino and other stone-masons, the imposing building was home to one of the city's foremost confraternities, honoured with an annual visit by the Doge. ✪ *Campo S Rocco, S Polo 2454 • Map K4 • Open Apr–Oct: 9am–5:30pm daily; Nov–Mar: 10am–4pm daily • Admission charge*

Campo San Giacomo dell'Orio

Named after either a bay tree, wolves or a canal depending on your source, this picturesque quintessential square, well off the beaten track, sports plane trees, benches for relaxing and patches of grass. Modest sur-rounding palaces are home to Venice University's architectural faculties. The laid-back air and abundance of eateries and coffee shops make it very inviting, and there's no lack of subjects for photographers or artists. ✪ *Map L2*

Chiesa di San Giacomo dell'Orio

On no account miss this unusual church. Founded in the 9th century, its Latin-cross shape boasts a marvellous 15th-century wood-beamed ceiling and a forest of colourful granite and black limestone columns from the Middle East, several of them loot from the Crusades. The floor merits close scrutiny for its multitude of fossils, while mem-orable paintings include Palma il Giovane's *Descent of Manna* (1580–81), left of the main altar, and a painted crucifix (1350) attributed to Paolo Veneziano. ⊗ *Campo S Giacomo dell'Orio, S Croce* • *Map L2* • *Open 10am–5pm Mon–Sat, 1–5pm Sun* • *Admission charge*

6 Scuola Grande di San Giovanni Evangelista

One way to get into this erstwhile confraternity headquarters is to attend an evening concert held in the high-ceilinged upstairs hall, as the building is rarely open to visitors. The monumental staircase was the work of Coducci and the priceless reliquary contains a fragment of the True Cross, presented to the Scuola in 1369. The spectacular *Miracles of the Cross* cycle of paintings commissioned of Gentile Bellini and associates is now in the Accademia Galleries *(see pp24–5)*. The exterior courtyard has a fine sculptured portal screen by Pietro Lombardo mounted with an eagle to symbolize St John. ⊗ *Campiello della Scuola, S Polo 2454* • *Map L3*

Scuola Grande di San Giovanni Evangelista

7 Palazzo Mocenigo

An 18th-century patrician palace whose richly furnished and frescoed rooms also have showcases of historic fabrics and costumes including lavishly embroidered waistcoats, fans, bodices and corsets. The Mocenigo family portrait gallery boasts a total of seven doges, topped in fame by Alvise I, the victor at the 1571 Battle of Lepanto against the Turks, which was crucial for the Republic. ⊗ *Salizzada S Stae, S Croce 1992* • *Map M2* • *Open Apr–Oct: 10am–5pm Tue–Sun; Nov–Mar: 10am–4pm Tue–Sun* • *Admission charge*

Giardino Papadopoli

8 Giardino Papadopoli

A leafy haven of twittering sparrows and flowerbeds close to Piazzale Roma and the car parks, these French-designed gardens date back to the 1800s when extravagant parties for the nobility were held here among exotic flowers and rare animals. Site of a demolished convent, it belonged to Corfu-born entrepreneurs, hence the Greek

Campo San Zan Degolà

ame. The public park was
greatly reduced in size when the
Rio Novo canal was excavated
1932–3. ◈ Map J3

9 **Campo San Zan Degolà**
People usually hurry through
this square en route to the bus
terminal, oblivious to its quiet
charm. Interest starts with the
curious loggia on the western
canal edge, then there's the
attractive plain church named for
San Giovanni Decollato or St
John the Beheaded, depicted
with flowing curly locks in a
stone *bas-relief* on the southern
wall. Inside the simple Veneto-
Byzantine building are lovely
13th-century frescoes, an
unusual survivor for damp old
Venice. ◈ Map L1 • Chiesa di San
Giovanni Decollato: open 10am–noon
Mon–Sat

10 **Ca' Pesaro Museo di Arte
Orientale**
While the neighbouring modern
art gallery in monumental Ca'
Pesaro (see p20) is sadly still
closed for long-term restructuring, the impressive Oriental
Art Collection is an eclectic mix
of 19th-century curiosities from
all over the Far East. Exhibits
include armour, porcelain and
costumes, dainty lacquerwork
boxes and musical instruments.
◈ Fondamenta Pesaro, S Croce 2076
• Map N1 • Open 8:15am–2pm Tue–Sun
• Admission charge

A Day in San Polo

Morning

🕐 Drink your fill of Tintoretto's dynamic paintings
at the **Scuola Grande di
San Rocco** (see p81)
before wandering east to
Campo San Polo (see
p81). Coffee is a must in
the square, either at one
of the local bars or at the
attractive **Antica Birraria
La Corte** (see p85).

It's not far from here to
Rialto Market (see pp28–
9) for late morning bargains
of fresh produce, often
nearing half price when
stall-holders are in a hurry
to shut up shop. If this has
worked up an appetite, a
Grand Canal-side lunch is
worth consideration at this
point. One of a string of
eateries displaying live
lobster and fish close to
Rialto Bridge is Ristorante
Florida. Winter diners sit in
heated see-through
"tents" so that views of
the canal are ensured
(Riva del Vin, S Polo 736
• 041 528 51 66 • Closed
Thu & Dec–Jan).

Afternoon

🕐 Make your way north and
explore the craft and gift
shops, lace, scarf and T-
shirt stalls along Ruga
Rialto and the old red-light
area of **Rio Terrà Rampani**
(see p48).

🕐 Try to end up in pretty
**Campo San Giacomo
dell'Orio** (see p81) for a
pre-dinner drink at Al
Prosecco wine bar (Campo
S Giacomo dell'Orio, S
Croce 1657/03 • 041 524
02 22 • Closed Sun). Ask
for the fruity red Refosco
from Friuli and *bocconcino
con mortadella di cinghiale*
(bite-sized roll with wild
boar slice).

Around Town – San Polo & Santa Croce

Left **Gilberto Penzo** Centre **Sabbie e Nebbie** Right **Hibiscus**

🔟 Craft Shops

1 Gilberto Penzo
A visit to this workshop with beautiful wooden models of traditional Venetian boats is a real treat. Many craft come in DIY kit form. ◈ *Calle II° dei Saoneri, S Polo 2702 • Map M3*

2 Mazzon le Borse
For 50 years Papa Piero has been personally making beautiful leather bags that last a lifetime. Luckily his daughter Marta is taking over the reins. ◈ *Campiello S Tomà, S Polo 2807 • Map L4*

3 Tragicomica
The result of 20 years of creating elaborate *papier-mâché* and leather masks and brocade costumes for Carnival as well as theatrical productions can be appreciated in this spectacular craft shop where the staff explain the significance of pieces. ◈ *Calle dei Nomboli, S Polo 2800 • Map M4*

4 La Zanze Venexiana
Thin handpainted wood bookmarks treated with gold leaf and colourful zodiac signs are among the curiosities to choose from in this tiny corner shop. ◈ *Ponte dei Frari, S Polo 2566 • Map L3*

5 Michele Cicogna
Looking for a Blackamoor lampstand, gilded cherub or a dresser adorned with Canaletto-style scenes? This vast showroom akin to a museum is the workshop of a skilled restorer. ◈ *Campo S Tomà, S Polo 2867 • Map L4*

6 La Pedrera
Handmade beads, photo frames and Murano glass creations. ◈ *Campo Sant'Agostin, S Polo 2279/a • Map L3*

7 Sabbie e Nebbie
Tasteful boutique of pottery, candles and oddities from Japan and Italy. ◈ *Calle dei Nomboli, S Polo 2768/a • Map M4*

8 Attombri
In an old covered passageway long home to the Rialto Market goldsmiths is a young designer who makes limited-edition necklaces. ◈ *Sottoportego degli Orefici, S Polo 74 • Map P2*

9 Hibiscus
A mix of Indian silk jackets, platters from Morocco and ceramic bowls by a Veneto artisan. ◈ *Ruga Rialto, S Polo 1060/61 • Map P2*

10 C'era
The name of the shop translates as "as it was", reflected here in candles moulded into the shape of fossils and Classical columns. ◈ *Campo delle Beccarie, S Polo 360 • Map N2*

For what to buy in Venice **See p69**

Price Categories

For a three-course	**€** under €30
meal for one with half	**€€** €30–€40
a bottle of wine (or	**€€€** €40–€50
equivalent meal), taxes	**€€€€** €50–€60
and extra charges	**€€€€€** over €60

Left **Da Crecola** Right **Taverna Da Baffo sign**

10 Places to Eat

1 La Zucca
Delicious vegetarian fare, with the promise of unforgettable chocolate desserts. ❧ *Ponte del Megio, S Croce 1762 • Map L1 • 041 524 1570 • Closed Sun • No disabled access • €€*

2 Da Crecola
Laid-back family-run pizzeria in a beautiful setting alongside a church and canal. ❧ *Campo del Giovan, S Croce 1459 • Map L1 • 041 524 1496 • No disabled access • €*

3 Al Nono Risorto
Lively eatery with youthful clientele and great pizzas served in the garden. ❧ *Sottoportego de la Siora Bettina, S Croce 2337 • Map K1 • 041 524 1169 • Closed Wed, Thu L • No credit cards • No disabled access • €€*

4 Al Ponte
Canalside setting and home-style Venetian cooking, such as *polpette* (meatballs). ❧ *Calle Larga San Giacomo dell'Orio, S Croce 1666 • Map L2 • 041 719 777 • Closed Sun • €€*

5 Ai Coghi
Unusual meats such as wild boar and ostrich, along with pizza and fish. ❧ *Rio Terà S Silvestro, S Polo 1022/A • Map N3 • 041 522 7307 • No disabled access • €€*

6 Frary's
A welcoming eatery whose menu features flavours from the Middle East. ❧ *Fondamenta dei Frari, S Polo 2559 • Map L3 • 041 720 050 • Closed Tue • No disabled access • €*

7 Antica Birraria La Corte
Delectable pizzas named after the city's bridges feature at this ultra-modern eatery set in a former brewery. There is also a pleasant, tree-shaded patio. ❧ *Campo S Polo, S Polo 2168 • Map M3 • 041 275 0570 • Closed Mon • €€*

8 Osteria Al Diavolo e l'Aquasanta
If the traditional Venetian tripe isn't to your fancy, try the bean and pasta *(pasta e fagioli)* soup, with *tiramisù* to finish. ❧ *Calle della Madonna, S Polo 561B • Map N2 • 041 277 0307 • Closed Tue • No disabled access • €€*

9 Taverna Da Baffo
Seek out this tranquil square for a light lunch with a glass of Belgian beer or crisp Friuli wine. ❧ *Campo della Chiesa, S Polo 2346 • Map L3 • 041 520 8862 • No disabled access • €*

10 Pasticceria Da Tos
Luscious chocolate eclairs and dainty almond pastries are served in this old-style cake shop. ❧ *Calle dei Saoneri, S Polo 2750 • Map M3 • No disabled access • €*

Note: Unless otherwise stated, all restaurants accept credit cards and serve vegetarian meals

Left **Zattere** Right **Squero di San Trovaso**

Dorsoduro

A DISTRICT OF CONTRASTS, *Dorsoduro stretches from the port, backed by an historic but rather run-down zone long home to sailors and fishermen, via the panoramic Zattere and Grand Canal, all the way to the Punta della Dogana, a chic area of foreign consulates and wealthy residences. Highlights for visitors include two foremost art galleries, the Accademia and the Peggy Guggenheim Collection, crammed with masterpieces ancient and modern, as well as Ca' Rezzonico palace and magnificent churches, Santa Maria della Salute and San Sebastiano, the latter famous for its wonderful Veronese canvases. Literally the "hard backbone" of Venice as it was built on elevated islands of compacted subsoil, Dorsoduro used to be sparsely populated due to its exposure to pirate attacks. Today, as home to most of the city's university premises, it is full of lively cafés, bars and nightlife, concentrated in the market square, Campo Santa Margherita.*

🔟 Sights

1. Accademia Galleries
2. Zattere
3. San Nicolò dei Mendicoli
4. Squero di San Trovaso
5. Chiesa di San Sebastiano
6. Rio Terrà dei Catecumeni
7. Ex Ospedale degli Incurabili
8. Campo San Barnaba
9. Chiesa dei Gesuati
10. San Basilio Port Zone

San Nicolò dei Mendicoli

Preceding pages **The domes of San Marco**

1 Accademia Galleries
See pp24–5.

2 Zattere
This broad waterfront took its name from the rafts of timber *(zattere)* floated downstream from the extensive forests in the northern Dolomite region which were managed by the Venetian Republic. The precious wood was used for constructing palaces or transformed into masts and the like for the important shipbuilding industry. The tall-masted sailing ships and rowing boats which used to moor here have been replaced by motorized *vaporetti* and tourist launches, and nowadays the Zattere signifies lovely lagoon views, perfect for a day or evening stroll. ◈ *Map C5*

3 San Nicolò dei Mendicoli
This Veneto-Byzantine church with an imposing square campanile (bell tower) will be recognized by film buffs from the chilling Nicholas Roeg film *Don't Look Now*. Hidden away in a maze of narrow alleyways off the port zone, "St Nicholas of the beggars" has a pretty portico which doubled as a shelter for the poor. Founded in the 7th century, it is the second oldest church in Venice. In the 1970s it was restored by the Venice in Peril Fund, who waterproofed the low floor.
◈ *Campo S Nicolò, Dorsoduro 1907 • Map A5 • Open 10am–noon, 4–6pm Mon–Sat, 9:30–11am, 4–6pm Sun • Free*

4 Squero di San Trovaso
This is by far the city's most famous gondola repair and construction yard, though its active days may be numbered. The combined workshop-dwelling, its window sills clad with geraniums, is reminiscent of an Alpine chalet as the first occupants came from the mountainous Cadore region. Though closed to visitors, it backs on to a canal (Rio di San Gervasio e Protasio) so it's easy to watch the goings-on as oar-propelled craft are brought in for caulking and cleaning. ◈ *Map C5*

5 Chiesa di San Sebastiano
This 16th-century church is a treasure trove of Paolo Veronese paintings, and the artist devoted most of his life to the spectacular fresco cycle *(see p39)*.
◈ *Campo S Sebastiano, Dorsoduro 1907 • Map B5 • 041 275 04 62 • Open 10am–5pm Mon–Sat • Admission charge*

6 Rio Terrà dei Catecumeni
This reclaimed thoroughfare between the Zattere and Santa Maria della Salute is dominated by a long building, now a school, where prisoners-of-war of the Republic who did not profess the Christian faith would be held captive until they converted. This quiet backwater comes alive on 21 November when the Salute festivities are in full swing and it's taken over by a carnival atmosphere *(see p63)*. ◈ *Map D5*

Ex Ospedale degli Incurabili façade

Boats moored at the San Basilio Port Zone

7 Ex Ospedale degli Incurabili

A cavernous, labyrinthine construction that takes up a lengthy stretch of the Zattere, this erstwhile hospital is undergoing vast renovations to adapt it for the Accademia Art Institute, scheduled to transfer here and leave the historic galleries room for expansion *(see pp24–5)*. The building dates from the 1500s, founded to shelter women with incurable venereal diseases, and later took in orphans and a trade school. Legend has it that St Francis Xavier, ordained in Venice, was sent to serve here with his companions on orders from Ignatius Loyola. More recently, it has served as a

---

Masks

Handmade in *papier-mâché* and glittery plaster, Venetian masks are now strictly tourist fare, but they were once essential attire during Carnival, allowing aristocrats to enjoy themselves in anonymity. One unusual model, with a long curved nose, was used by doctors during plagues, its cavity filled with perfumed herbs to filter the diseased air.

---

juvenile court. ◈ *423 Zattere, Dorsoduro 30135 • Map C5 • Closed to public*

8 Campo San Barnaba

Nowadays a modest square dotted with some low-key bars, its main attraction is a colourful moored barge loaded high with shiny fresh fruit and vegetables – a must for photographers. Its history has not always been so peaceful, however – the square used to be the arena for fierce rivalries between the city's working class bands, the Nicolotti and Castellani, who would fight it out on the Ponte dei Pugni *(see p47)*. On a more forgiving note, the rather nondescript church used to take in disgraced and bankrupt nobility. ◈ *Map K5*

9 Chiesa dei Gesuati

Set right on the Zattere waterfront close to the main ferry moorings, the Gesuati (also known as Santa Maria del Rosario) is often confused with the Gesuiti (Jesuit) establishment in Cannaregio. Taking over from a minor religious order, the Domenican friars had this church constructed in Classical style in 726 by Giorgio Massari. Inside he ceiling consists of three uplifting frescoes (1737–9) by Tiepolo *(see p44)*, which are considered among his best work, portraying St Dominic amid glorious angels in flight. ◈ *Fondamente delle Zattere, Dorsoduro 864 • Map C5 • Open 9am–6pm Mon–Sat, 1–6pm Sun • Admission charge*

10 San Basilio Port Zone

The vast docks occupy a good part of the northwestern continuation of the Zattere waterfront, and are usually crowded with trucks and cars queueing up to board the ferries to Greece. The modern terminal also handles the increasing cruise liner traffic, whereas the former industrial structures such as the cotton mill and cold stores are being converted for use by Venice University *(see p54)*. The outstanding 17th-century pastel portrait artist Rosalba Carriera *(see p25)* was born in the San Basilio parish and returned there to die, destitute and totally blind, in 1757. ◈ *Map B5*

Statue in Chiesa dei Gesuati

Exploring Dorsoduro

Morning

🕐 The **Accademia Galleries** *(see pp24–5)* can be overwhelming, so focus on a selection of its glories, but don't neglect the Carpaccios and Bellinis. After all that art, have a relaxing coffee watching the boats go by at Snack Bar Accademia Foscarini, a magical spot right at the foot of Accademia Bridge. *(Rio Terrà Antonio Foscarini, Dorsoduro 878/C • 041 522 72 81 • Closed Tue).*

Next, head off east for a leisurely stroll, past Longhena's work of art, the church of **Santa Maria della Salute** *(see p38)*, to Punta della Dogana, a great spot for taking photos of Piazza San Marco. Turn back in the direction of the Zattere and Giudecca Canal. Lunch is recommended at Al Chioschetto, a snack bar right on the water's edge. *(Zattere, Dorsoduro 1406/a • 338 117 40 77).*

Afternoon

Wander through to **Campo Santa Margherita** *(see pp32–3)* to the Scuola Grande dei Carmini to admire Tiepolo's canvases, then take time to admire the architectural curiosities of this fascinating square.

As sunset approaches waste no time in occupying a table for a Spritz apéritif at the trendy bar Margaret DuChamp *(Campo S Margherita, Dorsoduro 3019 • 041 528 62 55).* It's hard to better this as a place for people-watching, and an added bonus is the scent of jasmine that fills the air as night falls.

Left **BAC Art Studio** Right **Totem-Il Canale Gallery sign**

TOP 10 Shops

1 869
Paola Carraro transforms paintings by modern masters Klee, Magritte and others into hand-knitted sweaters and dresses. Commissions are taken so you can wear your favourite painting. ® *Piscina del Forner, Dorsoduro 869 • Map D5*

2 Bac Art Studio
Attractive and affordable etchings and prints of Venice by artists Baruffaldi and Cadore. Buy them framed if desired. ® *Piscina del Forner, Dorsoduro 862 • Map D5*

3 Totem-Il Canale Gallery
Bulky ancient beads, made with vitreous paste and once traded in Africa, are now precious antiques. Contemporary African wood artworks as well. ® *Rio Terrà Antonio Foscarini, Dorsoduro 878/B • Map C5*

4 Signor Blum
Detailed jigsaw models of Gothic palaces, flanked by wall panels and painted toy figures all individually handmade by this co-operative of female artisans. ® *Campo S Barnaba, Dorsoduro 2840 • Map K5*

5 Danilo Mazzon
Everyone's Christmas tree needs one of the joyous gilded cherubs lovingly crafted by wood-carver and painter Danilo. He also makes picture frames and furniture. ® *Ponte S Barnaba, Dorsoduro 2808 • Map K5*

6 La Bottega del Vasaio
Replicas of Renaissance vases and tiles are fashioned by this talented young ceramist. ® *Campo S Margherita, Dorsoduro 2904 • Map K5*

7 Ca' Macana
Mask-makers extraordinaire, with life-size unicorns, pointy jester heads with bells and the full Carnival range. ® *Calle delle Botteghe, Dorsoduro 3172 • Map L5*

8 Billa Supermarket
Open seven days a week with freshly baked bread, great cheese and salami counter, wine, fruit and vegetables. ® *Zattere, Dorsoduro 1491 • Map D5*

9 Giovanni Moro
Miniatures of Venice's palaces and bridges modelled by the craftsman who has produced a 6 x 4m (20 x 13 ft) model of the entire city. ® *Calle della Toletta, Dorsoduro 1193 • Map L6*

10 Capricci e Vanità
Lovely antique lace table-cloths and accessories, such as 1920s-style bead bags, on sale in this tasteful boutique. ® *S Pantalon, Dorsoduro 3744 • Map K4*

For more on shopping in Venice **See p138**

Price Categories	
For a three-course meal for one with half a bottle of wine (or equivalent meal), taxes and extra charges	€ under €30
	€€ €30–€40
	€€€ €40–€50
	€€€€ €50–€60
	€€€€€ over €60

Left **Gelateria Nico** Right **Da Mortin**

10 Places to Eat

1 Gelateria Nico
Venice's most renowned ice cream parlour. The local favourite is *giandiuotto da passeggio*, a slab of hazelnut and chocolate ice cream smothered in whipped cream. ◈ *Zattere, Dorsoduro 922 • Map D5 • 041 522 5293 • Closed Thu • €*

2 Alla Toletta
Choose from an innovative range of pizza slices to take away, including wild mushroom, smoked ham, tomatoes and rocket. ◈ *Calle della Toletta, Dorsoduro 1309 • Map L6 • 041 523 6518 • €*

3 Pizzeria ai Sportivi
Easily the best pizza in Venice, with delicious toppings of Treviso radicchio or porcini mushrooms. Outdoor seating. ◈ *Campo S Margherita, Dorsoduro 3052 • Map K5 • 041 521 1598 • €*

4 Bar Abbazia
Shaded by a leafy pergola, the outside tables are perfect for enjoying a quick sandwich. ◈ *Rio Terrà dei Catecumeni, Dorsoduro 128-129/A • Map D5 • 041 523 2149 • €*

5 Osteria da Codroma
Poetry readings and live music are often staged in this timber-panelled *osteria*. ◈ *Fondamenta Briati, Dorsoduro 2340 • Map B4 • 041 524 6789 • Closed Thu • €*

6 Da Montin
Popular with the art world since the 1950s, the walls of this restaurant are decorated with modern art. Cool, creeper-shaded garden. ◈ *Fondamenta delle Eremite, Dorsoduro 1147 • Map B5 • 041 522 7151 • Closed Wed • €€€*

7 Suzie Café
This great bar, frequented by students, serves sandwiches, pasta and salads. ◈ *Campo S Basilio, Dorsoduro 1527 • Map B5 • 041 522 7502 • Closed Sat–Sun • €*

8 Ai Gondolieri
One of the city's top restaurants, specializing in game from the Veneto when in season. Extensive wine list. ◈ *Ponte del Formager, Dorsoduro 366 • Map D5 • 041 528 6396 • Closed Tue • €€€€€*

9 Pasticceria Tonolo
One of the city's best pastry shops. Delicious, freshly baked almond biscuits and mini pizzas are recommended. ◈ *Crosera S Pantalon, Dorsoduro 3764 • Map K4 • 041 523 7209 • Closed Mon • €*

10 Gelateria Il Doge
Try *Zuppa del doge* (candied fruit, egg custard and sponge cake soaked in Marsala) at this great ice cream parlour. ◈ *Campo S Margherita, Dorsoduro 3058A • Map K5 • 041 523 4607 • Closed Nov–Jan • €*

Note: Unless otherwise stated, all restaurants accept credit cards and serve vegetarian meals

Left **La Cantina** Right **Fondamenta degli Ormesini**

Cannaregio

ACCOUNTING FOR THE HUGE CRESCENT between the northern bank of the Grand Canal and the lagoon, the bustling sestiere of Cannaregio reaches from the railway station to the city hospital. It was home to Marco Polo and artists Titian and Tintoretto, and boasts landmark churches such as Madonna dell'Orto along with an old Jewish Ghetto. Named after the reeds (canne) that once filled its marshes, it is crossed by Strada Nova, the city's main thoroughfare, but also boasts Venice's narrowest alley, the 58-cm (2-ft) wide Calle Varisco. Never a dull moment passes thanks to its market, craft workshops and rowing clubs, while relaxation comes at the string of shady parks and laid-back cafés and bars that line the maze of back-street canals.

🔟 Top 10 Sights

1. Ca' d'Oro
2. Jewish Ghetto
3. Corte Seconda del Milion
4. Santa Maria dei Miracoli
5. Campo dei Mori
6. Farmacia Ponci
7. Fondamente della Misericordia and degli Ormesini
8. Palazzo Labia
9. Chiesa di San Giobbe
10. Fondamente Nuove

Chiesa di San Giobbe

1 Ca' d'Oro

Behind the palace's beautiful Gothic tracery is a memorable column-filled courtyard paved with myriad coloured *tesserae*. Inside is the Galleria Franchetti, an enticing collection of paintings, sculptures, coins and ceramics donated to the State by Baron Giorgio Franchetti in 1916, together with the building. One highlight is Andrea Mantegna's agonizing *St Sebastian* (1560) pierced by arrows "like a hedgehog", in the portico leading through to a stunning loggia overlooking the Grand Canal. An ornate 15th-century staircase climbs to the second floor where there are huge 16th-century Flemish tapestries *(see p42)*. ✆ Calle Ca' d'Oro, Cannaregio 3932 • Map N1 • Open 8:15am–1:30pm Mon, 8:15am–7:15pm Tue–Sun • Admission charge

2 Jewish Ghetto

The word "ghetto" originated in Venice, derived from *getto* (casting) due to an old iron foundry here. As of 1492 many Jewish refugees reached Venice after expulsion from Spain and in 1527 they were obliged by law to move to this area. Subject to a curfew to prevent their fraternizing with local women, they slept behind locked gates, their island circled by an armed patrol boat. Waves of arrivals saw each language group build its own synagogue (five in all) and raise the low-ceilinged buildings to seven floors in height. Today 33 Jews still live in the ghetto, while a further 450 reside in other parts of the city. The synagogues can be visited with a guide and there's a museum of sacred objects. ✆ Museo Ebraico, Campo del Ghetto Nuovo, Cannaregio 2902/b • Map C1 • Open Jun–Sep: 10am–7pm Sun–Fri; Oct–May: 10am–4:30pm Sun–Fri • Admission charge

3 Corte Seconda del Milion

The newly restructured Malibran Theatre in this photo-genic square was erected on the site of the Polo family abode, where famous 13th-century explorer Marco was born *(see p52)*. Other early Gothic buildings remain, their timber overhangs set off by bright red geraniums. Along with the adjoining bridge, the square was named in honour of the explorer whose marvellous stories about the Orient in his book *Il Milione* continue to inspire generations of travellers. ✆ Map Q2

Moor sculpture

4 Santa Maria dei Miracoli

A "jewellery box" of marble slabs and exqui-site *bas-reliefs*, this Renaissance church was named after a miracle-working icon from 1409, said to have resuscitated a drowned man and now enshrined in the main altar *(see p38)*. ✆ Campo dei Miracoli, Cannaregio • Map Q2 • 041 275 04 62 • Open 10am–5pm Mon–Sat, 1–5pm Sun • Admission charge

5 Campo dei Mori

In this odd funnel-shaped square your attention is drawn to three statues of Arabian-style "Moors" – but neither North African nor Muslim, they hailed from Morea in Greece. Rioba, Sandi and Afani Mastelli were medieval traders who made

Medicinal potions, Farmacia Ponci

their home in the family palace around the corner. Next to the bridge over Rio della Sensa is a doorway marked No. 3399, once the residence of the renowned 16th-century artist Tintoretto *(see p44).* ◈ *Map D1*

6 Farmacia Ponci
The "Casa degli Speziali", the oldest pharmacy in Venice, carries on its business in modern premises alongside its restored 16th-century rooms. Displayed on original briarwood shelving adorned with Baroque statues in Arolla pinewood, are rows of 17th-century porcelain jars for medicinal ingredients; for safety reasons poisons were kept in a rear room. Pharmacies were strictly regulated and totalled 518 in 1564, the year their guild was formed. ◈ *Strada Nova, Cannaregio 2233A • Map P1*

7 Fondamente della Misericordia and degli Ormesini
Parallel to the Strada Nova but worlds away from the tourist bustle, these adjoining quaysides have a real neighbourhood feel. There's a good sprinkling of *osterie* (wine bars) alongside

Mexican and Middle Eastern restaurants, a continuation of former trade links: the word "*ormesini*" derives from a rich fabric traded through Hormuz, now in Iran, and imitated in Florence and Venice. Ormesini leads into Misericordia and to the towering red-brick Scuola Grande building. Currently closed for restructuring, it served as the city's basketball team headquarters for many years. ◈ *Map C2*

Palazzo Labia façade

8 Palazzo Labia
The fames and fortunes of this 17th-century palace over-looking the Canal di Cannaregio could fill a book. Abandoned when its wealthy merchant owners fled to Vienna at the fall of the Republic, it acted as a silk factory, saw-mill and primary school, but the worst damage was inflicted in 1945 when a boat loaded with munitions blew up right in front of it. Luckily the wonderful ballroom frescoed by Tiepolo has been restored. The palace now belongs to RAI, the Italian state broadcasting service. ◈ *Campo S Geremia, Cannaregio • Map C2 • Ballroom: open 3–4pm Wed–Fri by appointment only*

9 Chiesa di San Giobbe

Set in a peaceful square, his church is a bit of a hotch-otch after undergoing numerous architectural modifications before was suppressed under Napoleon. An oratory and a paupers' hospital, it was founded in the 14th-century, with funding from Doge Cristoforo Moro and decorations by Pietro Lombardo. Superb altarpieces by Giovanni Bellini and Vittorio Carpaccio now hang in the Accademia Galleries (see pp24–5), but still here are a 1445 triptych by Vivarini in the sacristy and a lovely *Nativity* (1540) by Girolamo Savoldo.

Campo S Giobbe, Cannaregio • Map C2 • Open 10am–noon, 3:30–5:30pm daily • Free

10 Fondamente Nuove

This lagoon-side pavement, opposite the cemetery island of San Michele (see p110), is an important jumping-off point for ferries to the northern islands and sports one of the city's rare petrol stations. The ample quaysides were not constructed and paved until the mid-1500s; until then the waterfront reached back to Titian's garden (No. 5113, Calle Larga dei Botteri) allowing him unobstructed views of the Alps on a clear day, which delighted this native of Cadore. • Map E2

The Jews in Venice

Banned by Republic law from practising manual trades, many Jews were skilled doctors or money-lenders. Most were refugees from other parts of Europe, and they are credited with introducing rice-based dishes to Venetian cuisine. As remembered by a memorial in the Ghetto, few returned from the Nazi camps of World War II.

Exploring Cannaregio

Morning

Begin the day with the Galleria Franchetti in the lovely **Ca d'Oro** (see p95), but leave plenty of time for the balconies which overlook the Grand Canal and the mosaics in the courtyard. Afterwards follow Strada Nova in the direction of the railway station to the Bottega del Caffè *(Calle del Pistor, Cannaregio 1903 • 041 714 232 • Closed Sat pm & Sun)* for the best coffee in Cannaregio. Only minutes away is the fascinating **Jewish Ghetto** *(see p95)*, where you can take a guided tour to the many remaining synagogues in the area.

For a revitalising break, lunch at Hostaria alla Fontana is recommended *(Fondamenta di Canna-regio, Cannaregio 1102 • 041 715 077 • Closed Sun & Mon am)*.

Afternoon

Wander up the canal towards **Ponte dei Tre Archi** (see p46) and the **Chiesa di San Giobbe**. Return back over the bridge and make your way to Fondamenta della Sacca, which affords good views of the Dolomites in clear conditions. Many ways lead east from here, but try and take in the church of **Madonna dell'Orto** (see p39) for the Tintoretto paintings, then **Campo dei Mori** (see p95).

Back on Strada Nova, an energetic young team awaits at La Cantina with a pre-dinner glass of wine from their north Italian range *(Strada Nova, Cannaregio 3689 • 041 522 82 58 • Closed Sun)*.

Left **Tàkalá** Right **Le Ragazze di Cima**

TOP 10 Specialist Shops

1 Tàkalá
Close to Campo SS Apostoli, a gift shop of fascinating holograms, Murano glass delights and chunky jewellery. ✎ *Strada Nova, Cannaregio 4391/C • Map D2*

2 Ceramiche 'al Bocal'
Pottery workshop run by a couple who produce a great assortment of blue-and-white hand-decorated platters, tiny cups for *grappa* and teapots. ✎ *Strada Nova, Cannaregio 2282 • Map D2*

3 San Leonardo Market
In the morning and late afternoon this area functions as a lively open-air produce market. In autumn the air is thick with the aroma of roasting chestnuts. ✎ *Rio Terrà San Leonardo • Map C2 • Mon–Sat*

4 Lili e Paolo Darin
Original handmade glass beads in brilliant hues and myriad shapes, window hangings and Christmas decorations. ✎ *Salizzada S Geremia, Cannaregio 317 • Map C2*

5 TSL Tessile San Leonardo
Few passers-by manage not to be tempted by the great value velvety bathrobes, cut-price bed linen and fluffy towels here. ✎ *Rio Terrà S Leonardo, Cannaregio 1318 • Map C2*

6 Le Ragazze di Cima
Need a bridal trousseau or just a swimming costume? Lingerie for all occasions in silk and other fabrics can be found here. ✎ *Strada Nova, Cannaregio 3683/84 • Map D2*

7 Salmoiraghi & Vigano
Italian spectacles are stylish and good value, and this well-reputed optometrist can make up prescription glasses the same day. ✎ *Strada Nova, Cannaregio 3928-3930 • Map D2*

8 Standa
Handy department store. Casual clothing for all the family and a food department with a good delicatessen counter – great for picnics. ✎ *Strada Nova, Cannaregio 3659 • Map D2*

9 Libreria di Demetra
Large bookshop minutes from the railway station open until midnight seven days a week. A good stock of literature in English. ✎ *Campo S Geremia, Cannaregio 282 • Map C2*

10 Principe
Branches of this women's fashion store can be found all over Venice. The latest in trendy designs at value prices. ✎ *Rio Terrà S Leonardo, Cannaregio 1332 • Map C2*

Price Categories		
For a three-course	**€**	under €30
meal for one with half	**€€**	€30–€40
a bottle of wine (or	**€€€**	€40–€50
equivalent meal), taxes	**€€€€**	€50–€60
and extra charges	**€€€€€**	over €60

Left **Meson España** Right **Osteria al Bacco**

🔟 Places to Eat

1 Meson España
Beautifully restored Spanish-style premises. Sangria and Spanish wines go perfectly with the *tapas* and *paella*. ◎ *Sottoportego del Tagiapiera, Cannaregio 3711 • Map D2 • 041 522 2060 • Closed Mon • No disabled access • €€*

2 Il Gelatone
Try ice cream maestro Michele's *bacio* (kiss) of hazelnut and chocolate. ◎ *Rio Terrà Maddalena, Cannaregio 2063 • Map D2 • 041 720 631 • No disabled access • €*

3 Brek
A self-service restaurant open from breakfast to dinner, everything prepared as you wait. ◎ *Lista di Spagna, Cannaregio 124 • Map B2 • 041 244 0158 • €*

4 Trattoria Pontini da Giada e Roberta
The set menu here is excellent value, or try the innovative salads and apple strudel. Lunch only. ◎ *Ponte delle Guglie, Cannaregio 1268 • Map C2 • 041 714 123 • €*

5 Bar Matteo
Commuters en route to the station frequent this bar, with an unbeatable range of sandwiches. Eat in or take away. ◎ *Ponte delle Guglie, Cannaregio 321–326 • Map C2 • Closed Sun • €*

6 Sahara
Delicious Arab fare at low prices, such as *Magluba*, a rice dish with almonds, pine nuts, minced beef and aubergine (eggplant). ◎ *Fondamenta della Misericordia, Cannaregio 2519 • Map D2 • 041 721 077 • No credit cards • No disabled access • €*

7 Antica Mola
Friendly family trattoria with a garden and canalside dining. ◎ *Fondamenta degli Ormesini, Cannaregio 2800 • Map C2 • 041 717 492 • Closed Aug • €€*

8 Pizza e poi
Oven-fresh take-away pizza, smothered with both traditional and innovative toppings. ◎ *Strada Nova, Cannaregio 2222 • Map D3 • 041 522 8671 • No disabled access • €*

9 Osteria Anice Stellato
Book ahead for this popular place serving fish, meat and a wonderful *zabaglione* dessert. ◎ *Fondamenta della Sensa, Cannaregio 3272 • Map C1 • 041 720 744 • €€*

10 Osteria al Bacco
Fish-only restaurant with a garden. Try the spicy *spaghetti alla busara*, with prawns, tomato and chilli. ◎ *Fondamenta delle Cappuccine, Cannaregio 3054 • Map C1 • 041 717 493 • Closed Mon, 2 weeks Jan • €€€*

Left **Riva degli Schiavoni** Right **San Pietro di Castello**

Castello

NAMED AFTER A CASTLE *possibly built here in Roman times, Castello is the "fishtail" of Venice. The western half of the district is crammed with* historic highlights such as the churches of SS Giovanni e Paolo and San Zaccaria. However, half of Castello is taken up with shipbuilding, focusing on the historic Arsenale. The tree-lined Giardini is the venue for the Biennale (see p102).

TOP 10 Sights

1. Riva degli Schiavoni
2. Hotel Danieli
3. Santa Maria della Pietà
4. Arsenale
5. San Pietro di Castello
6. Campo Santi Giovanni e Paolo
7. Campo Santa Maria Formosa
8. Via Garibaldi & Giardini
9. Chiesa di San Francesco della Vigna
10. Ospedaletto

Statue, Santa Maria Formosa

1 Riva degli Schiavoni

Thronging with tour groups and packed with souvenir stalls, this quayside affords a lovely promenade past majestic palaces (now mostly hotels) and a much photographed 1887 monument to the first king of Italy, Vittorio Emanuele. It is linked to Piazza San Marco by the elegant Istrian stone bridge Ponte della Paglia, named after the straw *(paglia)* once unloaded from barges here. This is also the best place for taking pictures of the Bridge of Sighs. At the eastern end is the Ca' di Dio ("house of God"), a 13th-century hospice for pilgrims en route to the Holy Land. ◈ *Map F4*

2 Hotel Danieli

An enchanting 15th-century palace with a pink Gothic façade set on the magnificent waterfront near Piazza San Marco. After a string of aristocratic proprietors, it was taken over in 1822 by Joseph da Niel, who turned it into a hotel with an illustrious guest list, including Dickens, Wagner and Ruskin. In the 1940s an annexe was added amid great controversy – since 1102 no dwelling over one floor had been allowed on the site. The redeeming feature of the new wing is the roof restaurant *(see p144)*.

Gothic arches, Hotel Danieli

3 Santa Maria della Pietà

Inextricably linked with the composer and musician Antonio Vivaldi, this Classical-fronted church belonged to the adjoining home for foundlings where he taught. Come to an evening concert to appreciate Tiepolo's uplifting ceiling fresco exalting music and the young orphan choristers, identifiable by their sprigs of pomegranate blossom. The interior has choir stalls to accommodate both the singers and nobility who were not expected to mingle with the commoners. ◈ *Riva degli Schiavoni, Castello 3700 • Map F4 • Open Jun–Sep: 9:30am–noon, 3:30–6:30pm daily • Free*

4 Arsenale

Aptly named after the Arab word *darsina'a* (house of industry), Venice's formidable Arsenale shipyards at one time employed an army of 16,000 to produce the fleets that sailed the Mediterranean, spreading the Republic's influence through trade deals and naval superiority. Justifiably proud of its innovative assembly-line system, the Arsenale could construct a galley in a matter of hours, notably in 1574 while the French king Henry III was enjoying a banquet. Ringed by walls and towers bearing the winged lion, some of its ancient docks and workshops are now being adapted as exhibition and performance venues *(see p54)*. The row of stone lions guarding the entrance hail from various Greek islands looted by Venetian commanders. ◈ *Castello 2148 • Map G3 • Open 10am– 5.50pm Mon–Sat; 11am–5.50pm Sun • Admission charge*

5 San Pietro di Castello

A sleepy island of grassy squares and boatyards, it is hard to imagine that Venice's religious headquarters were centred here right up until 1807, when the Basilica San Marco became the city's cathedral. Linked to the rest of Castello by two broad bridges, San Pietro attracts artists for its evocative forlorn air and fun-lovers for the animated late-June neighbourhood fair. Art lovers also come for the church with work by Veronese and Coducci, flanked by the patriarchal palace-cum-army barracks.
◈ *Chiesa di San Pietro di Castello • Map H4 • Open 10am–5pm Mon–Sat, 1–5pm Sun • Admission charge*

6 Campo Santi Giovanni e Paolo

Dominated by the brick façade of the Gothic church SS Giovanni e Paolo, this breezy square welcomes visitors with a flotilla of outdoor cafés. Worthy of contemplation is one of the world's most magnificent equestrian statues, a stylized 15th-century portrait of the great *condottiere* Bartolomeo Colleoni. He left a legacy to the city on the condition that his statue be erected in front of San Marco, craftily "interpreted" by the governors as the Scuola Grande di San Marco close at hand. Gracefully

Tree-lined avenue in the Giardini

decorated with arches and *tromp l'oeil* panels by the Lombard masters, the former confraterni serves as the public hospital.
◈ *Map E3*

7 Campo Santa Maria Formosa

A lovely rounded church on this sun-blessed square appears to spread in all directions, the resu of a 7th-century bishop's vision of the "shapely" *(formosa)* Virgi Mary's request it be built where "a white cloud came to rest". Ar works are by Vivarini and Palma Vecchio. The square is a good place for a picnic or a game of football, in lieu of the bullfights and re-enactments of Venice's conquests held here in olden days. ◈ *Chiesa di Santa Maria Formosa • Map E3 • Open 10am–5pm Mon–Sat, 1–5pm Sun • Admission charge*

8 Via Garibaldi and Giardin

A pleasant avenue now lined with cafés and a market, Via Garibaldi was triumphantly name when the eponymous general marched into Venice in 1866 as part of his round-Italy campaign for Unification. Take a stroll to the Giardini (public gardens). To make way for the park in 1807, architect Selva *(see p45)* demolished four churches and convents and a sailors' hospice.
◈ *Map H5*

The Venice Biennale

The Giardini and its beautiful tree-lined avenues were inaugurated as an international exhibition area in 1895 under the entrepreneur Count Volpi di Misurata. Every two years more than 50 countries send artists to represent them, each with their own pavilion custom-designed by leading architects such as Alvar Aalto, Carlo Scarpa and James Stirling.

9 Chiesa di San Francesco della Vigna

In the back alleys of Castello, this Franciscan church sports a combination of architectural styles courtesy of both Sansovino and Palladio *(see p45)*, who designed the façade. The colonnaded cloister can be seen while you're appreciating Giovanni Bellini's *Madonna and Child* (1507). Playgrounds have replaced the 13th-century vineyards *(vigna)*. ◉ *Campo S Francesco della Vigna, Castello 6691 • Map F3 • Open Apr–Oct: 9am–12:30pm, 3–6pm Mon–Sat, 3–6:30pm Sun; Nov–Mar: 8am–12:30pm, 3–7pm Mon–Sat, 3–6:30pm Sun • Free*

10 Ospedaletto

For John Ruskin the sculptures on the façade of this almshouse church represented "masses of diseased figures and swollen fruit". Judge Longhena's work yourself, then pass through the church to the Sala della Musica. Female wards of the orphanage gave concerts in this pretty room embellished with 18th-century frescoes. ◉ *Barbarie delle Tole, Castello 6691 • Map F3 • Open Apr–Oct: 3:30–7pm Thu–Sat; Nov–Mar: 3–6pm Thu–Sat • Admission charge*

Longhena sculptures, Ospedaletto

A Day in Castello

Morning

After a visit to the Gothic church on **Campo Santi Giovanni e Paolo**, wander through the city's hospital. Although it is now ultra-modern inside, you can still appreciate the wonderful Renaissance façade, and a series of ancient courtyards and confraternity buildings. Continue the historic theme with a coffee and cake at old-style Rosa Salva *(Campo SS Giovanni e Paolo, Castello 6779 • 041 522 79 49)*.

Take a stroll, via **Campo Santa Maria Formosa**, to Campo San Zaccaria and the church with its Bellini painting and **Scuola di San Giorgio degli Schiavoni** *(see p40)* for its Carpaccio works. For lunch, **Via Garibaldi** is a good bet, at one of the cafés or at Sottoprova *(041 520 64 93 • Closed Mon)*.

Afternoon

Head east along Via Garibaldi, and detour briefly into the shady avenue for the statue of Giuseppe Garibaldi and his followers. After a visit to the island of **San Pietro di Castello**, make your way back via the lagoon and the **Giardini**. A poignant sculpture to the female partisans of World War II can be seen at water level.

Heading in the direction of San Marco, just past the mouth of Via Garibaldi, on the embankment is Angiò Bar, the perfect spot for a Venetian sunset together with a good glass of wine, not to mention all manner of delicious snacks *(Riva di S Biasio, Castello 2142 • 349 073 09 00)*.

Left **Pastificio Le Spighe** Right **Chips and Colours**

10 Specialist Shops

1 Spazio Legno
In a workshop close to the Arsenale *(see p54)*, craftsman Saverio Pastor sculpts traditional Venetian oars and rowlocks from walnut. Postcards, books and models also on sale. ⊗ *Ponte Storto di S Martino, Castello 3546/a • Map G3*

2 Pastificio Le Spighe
A normal grocery store at first sight, this hive of industry produces a marvellous range of homemade pasta and stocks gourmet olive oils and olive paste. ⊗ *Via Garibaldi, Castello 1341 • Map H5*

3 Chips & Colours
Original printed Venice T-shirts and cloth bags are on sale in an old bakery re-used as an internet point and art gallery. ⊗ *Via Garibaldi, Castello 1592 • Map H5*

4 Il Papiro
Tempting gifts in the shape of marbled paper-covered boxes, greeting cards and writing paper with artistic letterheads. ⊗ *Calle delle Bande, Castello 5275 • Map F4*

5 Anticlea Antiquariato
Inviting boudoir filled with an amazing collection of glass beads and striking hat pins. Necklaces and earrings can be made up on the spot. ⊗ *Calle S Provolo, Castello 4719/A • Map F4*

6 Mistero Atelier
Glorious Oriental emporium with a range of dazzling Thai and Indian silks made up to Italian

designs for suits, scarves and ties. ⊗ *Ruga Giuffa, Castello 4925 • Map E3*

7 Crovato
Contemporary light fittings in bold Italian designs and a great selection of coloured candles. ⊗ *Ruga Giuffa, Castello 4920 • Map E3*

8 Corte delle Fate
Ultra-modern footwear and zany accessories in the shape of bags, jewellery and garments for the young. ⊗ *Salizzada S Lio, Castello 5690 • Map E3*

9 Lanterna Magica
A toy and gadget shop where you can browse among star-studded umbrellas and "magic lantern" lamps with a procession of shadow figures. ⊗ *Calle delle Bande, Castello 5379 • Map F4*

10 SU.VE Supermarket
Freshly baked rolls, cheese and cold meats sliced individually and the usual food and household needs for self-catering tourists. ⊗ *Salizzada S Lio, Castello 5601 • Map E3*

Left **Trattoria Giorgione** Right **Alla Rivetta**

Price Categories	
For a three-course meal for one with half a bottle of wine (or equivalent meal), taxes and extra charges	**€** under €30 **€€** €30–€40 **€€€** €40–€50 **€€€€** €50–€60 **€€€€€** over €60

10 Places to Eat

1 Taverna Olandese Volante
Lively bar serving draught beer and where the rolls are named after pirates and the salads after ships – try the "Galeone" with prawn and hard-boiled egg. ◉ *Campo S Lio, Castello 5658 • Map E3 • 041 528 9349 • €*

2 Antica Pasticceria Venexiana
Wonderful savoury pastries and mini pizzas, for stand-up consumption at the bar or take-away. ◉ *Calle del Caffettier, Castello 6645 • Map E • 041 522 4483 • Closed Mon • €*

3 Boutique del Gelato
There's inevitably a queue outside this popular *gelateria*. Try the tangy *limone* (lemon) or *fragola* (strawberry) ice cream or creamy *gianduiotto* (hazelnut-chocolate). ◉ *Salizzada S Lio, Castello 5727 • Map E3 • 041 522 3283 • Closed Dec–Jan • €*

4 Osteria da Dante (Alle Alpi)
Low-ceilinged wine bar whose tables seem permanently occupied by card-playing men. Traditional counter fare such as *ovoleti* and *garusoli* (types of snails) and grilled sardines. ◉ *Corte Nova, Castello 277 • Map F3 • 041 528 563 • Closed Sun • €*

5 Trattoria Giorgione
After serving his fish specialities, owner Lucio entertains guests with Venetian folk songs. ◉ *Via Garibaldi, Castello 1533 • Map H5 • 041 522 8727 • Closed Wed • €€*

6 Alla Rivetta
Friendly eatery with a wonderful window display that may include octopus salad or scallops. ◉ *Ponte S Provolo, Castello 4625 • Map E4 • 041 528 7302 • Closed Mon • €€*

7 Alla Mascareta
A rustic bar for wine lovers accompanied by rolls and salads. ◉ *Calle Lunga S Maria Formosa, Castello 5183 • Map E3 • 041 523 0744 • €*

8 Alle Testiere
Tiny non-smoking restaurant with an unusual selection of fish, cheese and wines. ◉ *Calle del Mondo Novo, Castello, 5801 • Map E3 • 041 522 7220 • Closed Sun • €€€*

9 Hostaria ae Do Porte
Wood-lined tavern where fish is grilled in view of diners. Lunch only. ◉ *Corte delle Due Porte, Castello 6492 • Map E3 • 041 520 8842 • €*

10 Al Covo
Sophisticated candlelit fish dining and north Italian wine list. ◉ *Campiello de la Pescaria, Castello 3968 • Map F4 • 041 522 3812 • Closed Wed–Thu, 20 Dec–20 Jan, 2 weeks Aug • €€€€*

> **Note:** *Unless otherwise stated, all restaurants accept credit cards and serve vegetarian meals*

Left **San Michele** Right **Forte di Sant'Andrea, Certosa**

The Northern Lagoon

THE NORTHERN LAGOON IS DOTTED WITH *mud flats and abandoned islands where rambling monasteries lie crumbling in the sun, backed by sweeping views of snow-capped mountains. Refugees from the mainland, fleeing the Huns, first settled on Torcello, which grew with the additional influx of influential religious orders. Today, however, only a handful of islands are still inhabited – glassmaking Murano is the most important, while Burano, Mazzorbo and Sant' Erasmo have skeletal populations of fishermen and market gardeners. Salt pans, such as Le Saline, were a source of employment until as late as 1913.*

Sights

1 Torcello
2 Burano
3 Murano
4 Mazzorbo
5 San Francesco del Deserto
6 San Michele
7 Sant' Erasmo
8 Lazzaretto Nuovo
9 Certosa
10 Treporti-Punta Sabbioni

Murano

Preceding pages **Backwater canal, Venice**

1 Torcello
See pp30–31.

2 Burano
A haven for artists, brightly painted houses, fish and lace-making are the pride of Burano. The islanders cherish an old legend about a faithful sailor who resisted the Sirens' call and was rewarded with a magnificent veil of magical foam for his bride, later worked into lace, a trade that brought worldwide fame and fortune to the isolated fisherfolk. These days, although old women still strain their eyes with patient stitches, many articles are in fact imported from the Far East. The island's dramatically leaning bell tower is visible from afar. ◈ *Ferry No. 12 from Fondamente Nuove • Map H1*

3 Murano
Long synonymous with glassmaking, Murano developed blowing and fusion techniques to extraordinary heights in the 1500s, and so closely guarded were the trade secrets that skilled crafts-men could migrate only under pain of death. Though Venice's glass monopoly lasted only until the 17th century, its fame lives on. A visit to the Glass Museum with its 4,000 exhibits is a must *(see p40)*. Don't be put off by the reps who invite tourists to see a furnace and showroom; it's a unique opportunity to watch the glassblowers at work and is free of charge. However, if you accept a free boat trip from San Marco to a glass factory, you're expect-ed to make your own way back by *vaporetto* if you don't buy any-thing. Glassmaking aside, Murano is a lovely place to wander around, with canals, alleyways and friendly islanders. ◈ *Vaporetto lines 41 & 42 from Fondamente Nuove or 71 & 72 from S Zaccaria or Piazzale Roma • Map G2*

Torcello basilica

4 Mazzorbo
This pretty island of cats exudes a tranquil air as locals tend their vineyards or artichoke fields. Wicker cages for fattening up *moleche* (soft-shelled crabs) hang on racks over the water and the produce can be sampled in the low-key *trattorias*. Amid the scattering of houses are bold modern council blocks painted in pastel hues, an admirable enter-prise. Mazzorbo has its own boat stop but is also joined to Burano by a timber footbridge. ◈ *Ferry No. 12 from Fondamente Nuove • Map H1*

5 San Francesco del Deserto
A short distance from Burano, this attractive island of cypress trees is home to a Franciscan monastery. According to legend it was founded by St Francis in person, on his way back from preaching missions in Egypt and Palestine in 1220. In May, clad in their brown habits and sandals, the monks attend the Vogalonga in their heavy-duty boat, to the delight of the Venetians *(see p62)*. ◈ *Taxi launch from Burano's landing stage • Map H1 • Monastery: open 9–11am, 3–5pm Tue–Sun • Donation*

Lagoon Flora and Fauna

The lagoon abounds in gilt-head bream, sea bass, clams, cuttlefish and crabs, which are all prey for wetland waterfowl such as swans, egrets, cormorants and the rare black-winged stilts. Sea lavender blooms on land masses, rock samphire clings to crumbling masonry, while glasswort thrives in the salt-ridden marshes.

6 San Michele

San Michele became the city cemetery in 1826, in the wake of a hygienic Napoleonic decree that the dead should be buried far from the dwellings of the living. Entry to the cemetery is via a lovely Gothic portal surmounted by St Michael at odds with a dragon, and through the monk's colonnaded cloister. But don't neglect to visit the pretty marble-façaded church next door, designed by Mauro Coducci in 1469 *(see p45)*. On All Souls' Day (2 November), the place is crowded with relatives paying a visit to their dear departed. However unless you're a famous resident like Ezra Pound, Stravinsky or Diaghilev, your bones are dug up after 10 years and placed in an urn to make room for someone else. ◈ Ferry Nos. 41 & 42 from Fondamente Nuove • Map G2 • Cemetery: open 7:30am–6pm daily

7 Sant' Erasmo

Unflattering jokes circulate about the inhabitants of Sant' Erasmo, with reference to in-breeding. However, no one would dare to question their ability to produce delicious asparagus and artichokes which prosper on the sandy soil and are a mainstay of Rialto Market *(see p28)*. Just over 4 km (2.5 miles) long and 1 km (0.5 miles) at the broadest point, Sant' Erasmo offers a tranquil countryside, praised enthusiastically by the Romans who built sumptuous villas here. A couple of rickety old motor cars occasionally bump along the lanes, but bicycles and boats are still the main form of transport. ◈ Ferry No. 13 from Fondamente Nuove • Map H2

8 Lazzaretto Nuovo

Across the water from Sant' Erasmo, up until the 1700s this island served as a quarantine station for merchant ships entering the lagoon and suspected of carrying the plague, together with members of the population under observation. The long building housed up to 10,000 people during the 1576 pestilence, while cargoes were fumigated with rosemary and juniper in temporary shelters. Later converted into a military stronghold, it now swarms with archaeology enthusiasts intent on unearthing its secrets and students attending summer camps. ◈ Ferry No. 13 from Fondamente Nuove • Map H2 • Tours Apr–Sep: 9:45am & 4pm Sat–Sun

Sant' Erasmo

eporti-Punta Sabbioni

Certosa

9 Inhabited by religious communities for more than 600 years, the "charterhouse" island went the way of many of its neighbours under occupation by French, Austrian and Italian forces, though currently as the property of the City Council, is slowly being cleaned up as a public park. Though there is no public boat service, it can be seen from *vaporetto* lines 71 and 72 as they circle eastern Castello. Also clearly visible from the Lido-Punta Sabbioni ferry are the impressive fortified ramparts of Sanmicheli's 16th-century Forte di Sant'Andrea, which faced any hostile vessels that dared to enter the lagoon unbidden. ⊗ *Map H2*

Treporti-Punta Sabbioni

10 These joint localities both cling to the promontory extending westward from the mainland – a continuous string of beach resorts equipped with spacious camp sites. Treporti is a pretty, sleepy backwater of canals while Punta Sabbioni ("big sandy point") is a busy bus-ferry terminal for summer holiday-makers. It came into being as sand accumulated behind the 1,100-m (3,600-ft) breakwater erected to protect the port mouth and littoral, and offers lovely seaside strolls. ⊗ *Ferry Nos. 12 & 14 from Lido or Burano • Map H1*

Sailing the Lagoon

Morning

To save money, buy a *laguna nord* day ticket *(see p135)* then take a *vaporetto* to **Murano** *(see p109)* to watch a glassmaking demonstration at a furnace or one of the workshops. Don't miss Murano's very own Grand Canal, before returning via Fondamenta Manin with its medieval porticoes for the turn-off towards the Faro (light-house) landing stage. Bar al Faro is a perfect place for coffee. *(Fondamenta Piave 20, Murano • 041 739 724 • Closed Sun).*

Take a ferry to **Burano** *(see p109)*. Either picnic on the famous Burano biscuits or lunch at Da Romano. A popular meeting place for artists, its speciality is *risotto Romano*, a rice dish flavoured with fish broth *(Piazza Galuppi 221, Burano • 041 730 030).*

Afternoon

Pop over to **Torcello** *(see pp30–31)* by ferry for the awe-inspiring Byzantine mosaics in the basilica. Climb the bell tower for unbeatable views of the lagoon, and the mountains if visibility is favourable.

Return to the water on a ferry south for **Treporti**, past low-lying islands and tidal flats. A stretch parallel to the sandy littoral separating the lagoon from the Adriatic Sea takes you to **Punta Sabbioni**, where a stopover is feasible for a drink on the jetty.

End the day sailing across the broad lagoon mouth, via the **Lido** *(see p115)*, back to **Piazza San Marco** *(see pp16–19).*

Left **La Murrina** Centre and right **Mazzega**

TOP10 Specialist Shops

1 Guglielmo Sent
This talented family has been crafting eye-catching coloured glass necklaces, photograph frames and clocks since 1923.
⊗ *Fondamenta Vetrai 8/a, Murano*
• *Map G2*

2 ArtStudio
Watch glass artist Davide Penso at work producing marvellous African-inspired glass beads.
⊗ *Fondamenta Rivalonga 48, Murano*
• *Map G2*

3 Manin 56
Striking etched bowls and slender wine glasses from Salviati flank international designer items in this wonderful collection.
⊗ *Fondamenta Manin 56, Murano • Map G2*

4 Sergio Tiozzo
A family concern where the ancient, intricate art of murrhine *(millefiori)* is practiced. Tiny glass flowers are melted together in a kiln to produce delightful dishes and lamps.
⊗ *Fondamenta Manin 45, Murano • Map G2*

5 Barovier & Toso
The world's oldest family of glassmakers, the Baroviers trace their ancestry back to the 13th century. They still produce stunning contemporary pieces.
⊗ *Fondamenta Vetrai 28, Murano • Map G2*

6 Mazzega
Vast showrooms display traditional and semi-modern glass designs with an emphasis on chandeliers and vases.
⊗ *Fondamenta da Mula 147, Murano*
• *Map G2*

7 La Murrina
The first shop you see as you disembark at Murano, this internationally known firm specializes in distinctive modern pieces
⊗ *Piazzale Colonna 1, Murano • Map G2*

8 Pastificio e Panificio Giorgio Garbo
Sample Burano's trademark vanilla-flavoured shortbread, *bussolai*, freshly baked in traditional rounds or "S" shapes
⊗ *Via S Mauro 336, Burano • Map H1*

9 Giovanna Vitturi
Signora Vitturi's delicate lace handkerchiefs are sewn on a traditional cylindrical cushion.
⊗ *Via S Mauro 332, Burano • Map H1*

10 Lidia Merletti d'Arte
While the front of the shop is an emporium of lace tablecloths, hand towels and mats the rear is a gallery with a priceless 18th-century wedding gown, a lace fan owned by Louis XIV and lace altarpieces. ⊗ *Via Galuppi 215, Burano • Map H1*

Lidia Merletti d'Arte

For more on shopping in Venice **See p138**

Price Categories

For a three-course	€	under €30
meal for one with half	€€	€30–€40
a bottle of wine (or	€€€	€40–€50
equivalent meal), taxes	€€€€	€50–€60
and extra charges	€€€€€	over €60

Left **Antica Trattoria alla Maddalena** Right **Al Gatto Nero**

10 Places to Eat

1 Trattoria Busa alla Torre, Da Lele

Dine inside under timber rafters or outside in the square. Start with soft-shelled *moleche* (crab) or ravioli filled with fish, but leave room for the nougat pastries. ⊗ *Campo S Stefano 3, Murano • Map G2 • 041 739 662 • No disabled access • €*

2 Panificio Giovanni Marcato

Cheap take-away lunch of slices of pizza smothered with tomato and olives, and *bussolà torte*, a molasses shortbread with candied fruit and chocolate. ⊗ *Fondamenta Rivalonga 16, Murano • Map G2 • 041 739 176 • €*

3 Osteria La Perla Ai Bisatei

Home-style cooking and house wine at very reasonable prices. The *fritto misto* seafood is superb. Open for lunch only. ⊗ *Campo S Bernardo 6, Murano • Map G2 • 041 739 528 • No credit cards • No disabled access • €*

4 Trattoria Valmarana

Stylish eating on a waterside terrace opposite the Glass Museum *(see p41)*. Try *granchio pazzo al forno* (crab baked with herbs) and the Veneto wines. ⊗ *Fondamenta Navagero 31, Murano • Map G2 • 041 739 313 • €€*

5 Trattoria Al Corallo

A popular, chaotic trattoria. Dine on fresh fish by the canal. ⊗ *Fondamenta Vetrai 73, Murano • Map G2 • 041 739 636 • €*

6 Trattoria ai Cacciatori

Cheaper and quieter than neighbouring Burano, here you can savour potato dumplings with crab and, in autumn, local game. ⊗ *Mazzorbo 23 • Map H1 • 041 730 118 • €*

7 Antica Trattoria alla Maddalena

Renowned for its spring artichokes and roast duck, this laid-back trattoria also serves a light, local white wine. ⊗ *Mazzorbo 7B • Map H1 • 041 730 151 • €*

8 Al Gatto Nero

Wonderful al fresco fish restaurant on a quayside, surrounded by Burano's colourful houses. ⊗ *Fondamenta Giudecca 88, Burano • Map H1 • 041 730 120 • No disabled access • €€*

9 Locanda Cipriani

Meals in this historic establishment are served on the terrace. The house speciality is *filetto di San Pietro Carlina* (baked John Dory with tomato and capers). ⊗ *Piazza S Fosca 29, Torcello • Map H1 • 041 730 150 • Closed Tue • No disabled access • €€€€€*

10 Ca' Vignotto

Book in advance to eat at this lovely farmhouse turned trattoria. Dishes may include dumplings with crab and artichokes or asparagus lasagne. ⊗ *Via Forti 71, S Erasmo • Map H2 • 041 528 5329 • Closed Tue • No disabled access • €*

> **Note:** *Unless otherwise stated, all restaurants accept credit cards and serve vegetarian meals*

Left **San Giorgio** Centre **San Lorenzo garden** Rght **San Servolo artist at work**

The Southern Lagoon and Venice Lido

THE SOUTHERN LAGOON ENJOYS *protection from the Adriatic Sea with
shifting sand spits long transformed into a permanent littoral, the
residential Lido, with the ongoing help of nature and man. The latter's effort.
date back to the 6th century, but the earth and wicker barriers have since
been modified into sturdy seawalls and massive parallel breakwaters at the
shipping entrances of San Nicolò, Alberoni and Chioggia. On the lagoon's
southwestern edge are fish farms and wild shallows where hunters and
fishermen still roam, well clear of the Valle Averto reserve run by the World
Wildlife Fund for Nature (WWF). Closer to Venice itself is a cluster of sizeable
islands such as majestic San Giorgio and populous Giudecca, then
diminutive land masses such as a lazaret, where plague victims were once
quarantined but which has now been re-adapted as a home for stray dogs, c
sanatorium acquired for private development as an exclusive resort, and
countless other evocative abandoned places.*

10 Sights

1. San Giorgio
2. Giudecca
3. Lido: San Nicolò
4. Lido: beach side
5. Lido: Malamocco
6. San Lazzaro degli Armeni
7. Santa Maria delle Grazie
8. San Servolo
9. San Pietro in Volta & Pellestrina
10. Chioggia

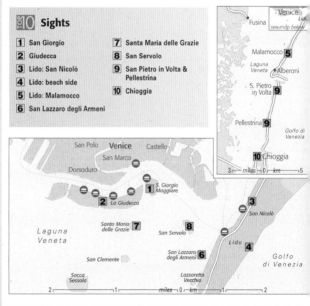

1 San Giorgio

The island of cypresses is physically separated from the main body of Venice by St Mark's Basin and retains a quiet meditative air, unconcerned with the bustle in the city. An ancient vineyard and salt pans were replaced by a landmark church by Andrea Palladio *(see p45)*, adjoining an elegant Benedictine monastery. It is now a scientific and cultural foundation and conference centre. At the rear is the open-air amphitheatre Teatro Verde, revived by the Biennale for performances of contemporary dance and music *(see p62)*.

Ⓢ *Fondazione Giorgio Cini (vaporetto No. 82)* • *Open Mon–Fri by appointment*

2 Giudecca

An S-shaped slice of land facing the sun-blessed Zattere, this residential garden island was first known as "Spina longa" for its fishbone form. It was renamed either after an early Jewish community, or the *giudicati* (radical aristocrats) exiled here. Renaissance artist Michelangelo spent three peaceful years here in voluntary exile from 1529. Much later it became an important industrial zone with shipbuilding and the immense Molino Stucky flour mill *(see p54)*. Usually quiet and neighbourly, it comes to life with a vengeance for the mid-July Redentore festivities *(see p62)*.

Ⓢ *Vaporetto Nos. 82, 41, 42*

3 Lido: San Nicolò

The northern end of the Lido littoral, a key point in the Republic's defence, used to be equipped with impressive naval fortifications and chains would be laid across the lagoon mouth as a deterrent to invaders. The historic Sensa celebration *(see p62)* is held offshore from the church of San Nicolò, founded in 1044 and a former Benedictine monastery, not far from the runway for light planes which offer tourist flights over Venice. One visitable site is the 1386 Jewish cemetery. Alternatively, take a 35-minute mini-cruise on the car ferry between Tronchetto car park and San Nicolò. Its high decks give great views all over Venice.

Ⓢ *Jewish Cemetery: Bus A from S Maria Elisabetta or car ferry from Tronchetto*
• *Guided visits in English 2.30pm Sun*
• *Admission charge*

4 Lido: beach side

Manicured sand raked daily and neat rows of multicoloured bathing cabins and beach umbrellas sum up the Lido from June to September, made famous in Thomas Mann's novel *Death in Venice (see p50)*. Venetians spend their summers socializing in style here. Things liven up considerably for the 10-day International Film Festival in September *(see p66)*, when the shady streets are filled with film buffs and critics on bicycles.

Ⓢ *Ferry lines Nos. 1, 6, 14, 51, 52, 61, 62*

Sunbathers, Lido beach resort

Heyday of the Lido

Evidence of the Lido's "golden age" as Europe's leading seaside resort at the turn of the 20th century can still be seen in the magnificent Art Deco villas. Exemplary survivors are the Hotel des Bains and the Excelsior, built in 1907 as the world's largest hotel, complete with mock minarets. Before that, the Lido was appreciated for its healthy air.

5 Lido: Malamocco

About midway along the Lido is the pretty, quiet village of Malamocco and it's now hard to imagine that it used to be the most important lagoon settlement soon after Roman times and the main port for Padua. A storm and giant waves washed away the entire town in 1106, later rebuilt in the vicinity on a smaller scale. It is appreciated for its 15th-century buildings, peaceful nature and rustic trattorias. *Bus No. 11 or line B from S Maria Elisabetta*

6 San Lazzaro degli Armeni

Venice made a gift of this erstwhile leper colony to the Armenian monk, the Venerable Mechtar, forced out of the Peloponnese during one of his country's *diasporas*. Intent on fostering the Armenian culture and language, he founded a religious community here and set up a printing press which operated until 1994, publishing works in 36 languages. Multi-lingual monks instruct visitors in their history and lead guided tours through a small museum and an impressive library of more than 100,000 volumes and precious illuminated manu-scripts. *Ferry line No. 20 from Riva degli Schiavoni • Open 3–5pm daily • Admission charge*

7 Santa Maria delle Grazie

Close to San Giorgio, this abandoned island used to be a hospice for pilgrims and was named after a miraculous image of the Virgin brought back from Constantinople and attributed to St Luke. Its colourful history features a series of religious orders and churches, devastating fires, allotments, luxuriant gardens and, until recently, the city's infectious diseases hos-pital. It is now private property with no public access.

8 San Servolo

In 1648, 200 nuns exiled from Candia by the Turks were lodged on this island, however after their numbers dwindled in 1725 it was given over to a sanatorium for psychiatric cases, although exclusively those of "comfortable circumstances". The roomy buildings are now shared by an international university and a trade school for artisans from all over Europe interested in restoration of traditional stone and stucco techniques. *Ferry No. 20 from Riva degli Schiavoni.*

Malamocco on the Lido

Traditional net-mending in Chioggia

9 San Pietro in Volta and Pellestrina

This narrow 11-km (6.5-mile) central strip of land, linked to the Lido and Chioggia by ferry, is dotted with picturesque sleepy fishing communities, once famous for lacemaking and now renowned for champion rowers and a shipyard. The Genoese wiped out the villages during the 14th century, an event almost repeated during the disastrous 1966 floods – powerful waves broke over the seawall, forcing full-scale evacuation. The massive defensive barriers with their 14-m (46-ft) broad base were first erected in the 1700s but have consequently needed large-scale reinforcement. ⊗ Bus No. 11 and ferry from the Lido or from Chioggia

10 Chioggia

A lively fishing town, with elegant bridges over navigable canals. The friendly inhabitants have a reputation for lawlessness and bickering, and speak a distinctive dialect with a singsong inflection. Chioggia has a rich history, but its greatest moment came as the arena for the decisive battle in the 1378–9 war, when the Genoese came close to conquering Venice. In flat-bottomed boats the crafty locals enticed the enemy into the lagoon, thus gaining the upper hand. ⊗ Ferry from Pellestrina or bus from Piazzale Roma

A Day on the Lagoon

Morning

From the Santa Maria Elisabetta ferry stop, either hire a bicycle or take buses B or V southwest along the lagoon edge for **Malamocco**. Wander through the peaceful village and over its bridge to the sea to take in the Adriatic and the impressive seawall. Then proceed with buses B or 11 through Alberoni and past the golf course for the vehicle ferry across the lagoon entrance. Get off at the second stop for **San Pietro in Volta**. Climb the high seawall for views of the sea, before turning lagoon-wards for the pastel-painted fishing settlement spread along the waterfront.

Have lunch at one of the trattorias (see p119) or a sandwich and glass of wine at Bar Susanna (Via Laguna 227 • 333 374 240).

Afternoon

Further south the bus terminates at **Pellestrina**, a brightly painted fishing village flanked by an active shipyard. The passenger ferry to **Chioggia** is a beautiful half-hour cruise past mussel grounds punctuated with fisher huts perched on poles, via the Ca' Roman landing stage, which provides access to a beach. Chioggia is a lovely town to explore, with its traffic-free piazza lined with old palazzos and countless fish restaurants.

Indulge in a pre-dinner drink and snack at Crema 13.06 Caffè, part of the ancient granary (Corso del Popolo 1306, Chioggia • 041 550 1082).

Left **Rizzo** Centre **Erbalido** Right **Arbor Boutique**

🔟 Shops and Markets

1 Rizzo
Unbeatable gourmet food from all over Italy – buffalo mozzarella, creamy Asiago cheese, cured Parma ham and gleaming olives. Pizza and *focaccia* can be found at the bread counter.
◎ *Gran Viale 18/20, Lido • Map H2*

2 General Market
Open-sided vans sell fresh produce daily, alongside designer-quality clothes, shoes and bags at approachable prices. Even if you don't buy anything, the lagoon setting looking over to the Venice skyline makes a trip worthwhile.
◎ *Via Falier, Lido • Map H2*

Confectionery at Rizzo

3 Erbalido
A traditional herbalist who can advise on natural remedies for minor ailments. ◎ *Via Negroponte 4/c, Lido • Map H2*

4 Arbor Boutique
The up-market range of mens- and womenswear attracts both foreign and Italian customers. ◎ *Santa Maria Elisabetta 10, Lido • Map H2*

5 Bruno Lazzari
This well-stocked bike shop rents out all normal steeds as well as 4-wheeler family models.
◎ *Viale Santa Maria Elisabetta 21/B, Lido • Map H2*

6 Standa-Oviesse
Department store with fashionable, moderately priced clothing for all ages, combined with a supermarket with a great selection of picnic products. ◎ *Gran Viale, Lido • Map H*

7 Labbra Rosse
Great bargains on last season's footwear, on the Lido's main shopping drag.
◎ *Gran Viale 79a, Lido • Map H2*

8 El Penelo
Giorgio Boscolo is an expert on traditional fishermen's clay pipes and the only craftsman still to make them in terracotta and coloured glazes.
◎ *Corso del Popolo 1355, Chioggia • Map F1*

9 Carlo Bullo
Ignore the trinkets here and focus on the handcrafted models of *bragozzo* boats *(see p22)* painted in primary colours.
◎ *Corso del Popolo 1350, Chioggia • Map F1*

10 Panificio Sergio
These dry biscuits were traditionally made for seafarers. *Pevarini* are spicy rings with molasses and aniseed, while *Dolce del Doge* is spread with a chocolate-hazelnut mixture.
◎ *Stradale Ponte Caneva 626, Chioggia • Map F1*

For more on shopping in Venice See p138

Price Categories

For a three-course	**€** under €30
meal for one with half	**€€** €30–€40
a bottle of wine (or	**€€€** €40–€50
equivalent meal), taxes	**€€€€** €50–€60
and extra charges	**€€€€€** over €60

Left **Harry's Dolci** Right **Los Murales**

🔟 Places to Eat

1 Altanella
Treat yourself to a candlelit dinner on the terrace. Fish dishes such as *frittura mista* (assorted fried seafood) are the speciality. Booking advisable. 🔊 *Calle delle Erbe, Giudecca 268 • Map E6 • 041 522 7780 • Closed Mon–Tue, Jan & Aug • No credit cards • No vegetarian options • No disabled access • €€€*

2 Harry's Dolci
With views across the Giudecca Canal, this is the "sweet" branch of Harry's Bar *(see p21)* serving sorbets and pastries. 🔊 *Fondamenta S Biagio, Giudecca 773 • Map E6 • 041 522 4844 • €€*

3 Los Murales
Lively Mexican eatery with outdoor seating, views over to San Marco and non-stop music. 🔊 *Fondamenta della Croce, Giudecca 68-71 • Map E6 • 041 523 0004 • No credit cards • No disabled access • €*

4 Trattoria Scarso
This good-value family eatery has a lovely garden hung with fishing nets where you can linger over grilled fish or a fresh salad. 🔊 *Piazzale Malamocco 5, Malamocco • Map H2 • 041 770 834 • Closed Tue, few weeks Jan • €*

5 Agriturismo Le Garzette
Locals celebrate family anniversaries here with the crispy *frittura di pesce* (fried fish). 🔊 *Lungomare Alberoni 32, Malamocco • Map H2 • 041 731 078 • Closed Mon–Thu, Dec–Feb • No credit cards • €*

6 Trattoria Da Nane
Memorable fish restaurant and terrace with panoramic views. Its speciality is a *pasticcio di pesce* (seafood lasagne). 🔊 *Via Laguna 282, S Pietro in Volta • Map H1 • 041 527 9110 • Closed Mon, mid-Nov–mid-Mar • No vegetarian options • No disabled access • €€*

7 Ristorante da Memo
A modest seafood restaurant with outdoor tables. The menu includes shrimps, eel and sole. 🔊 *Via Laguna 157, Portosecco (S Pietro in Volta) • Map H1 • 041 527 9125 • Closed Tue • No disabled access • €*

8 Ristorante La Sgura
An enchanting setting on a quiet canal, this fish restaurant also does pizzas in the evening. Try the *zuppa di pesce* (fish soup). 🔊 *Fondamenta Marangoni 1295, Chioggia • Map F1 • 041 403 232 • Closed Mon • No vegetarian options • €*

9 Pizzeria Vecio Foghero
In a quiet courtyard through a portico. The patriotic *Pizza al tricolore* is topped with mozzarella, rocket (arugula) and tomatoes. 🔊 *Calle Scopici 91/B, Chioggia • Map F1 • 041 404 679 • Closed Tue • €*

10 Ristorante al Buon Pesce
Roomy and friendly family-style fish restaurant with a delicious range of fresh grilled fish or fried seafood. 🔊 *Stradale Ponte Caneva 625, Chioggia • Map F1 • 041 400 861 • Closed Wed, Dec • No vegetarian options • €*

Note: *Unless otherwise stated, all restaurants accept credit cards and serve vegetarian meals*

Left **Bo University, Padua** Right **Ponte Scaligero, Verona**

Padua, Vicenza and Verona

A WEALTH OF ART CITIES PUNCTUATES *the fertile Veneto plain that stretches in a broad wedge north from the Po River to the foothills of the Dolomites. There is ample evidence of the presence of Romans and Venetians alike in the shape of fascinating amphitheatres and elegant palaces in places such as Verona and Vicenza, both towns recently declared World Heritage Sites by UNESCO. Moreover, amid vineyards of grapes pressed for light sparkling Prosecco and aromatic Bardolino are charming, little visited villas with ornamental gardens. Each town has its distinctive character: business-like Padua, yet with a richly artistic and religious heart; Vicenza, contained and proper in its country setting and equally famous for its goldsmiths and the architecture of Andrea Palladio; then romantic Verona lazing on the banks of the mighty Adige River as it flows south swollen with snow-melt from the Alps. Highlights in each locality are all feasible as day-trips from Venice by train.*

🔟 Sights

1. Cappella degli Scrovegni
2. Bo University
3. Basilica del Santo
4. Piazza dei Signori
5. Teatro Olimpico
6. Palazzo Leoni Montanari
7. Verona Arena
8. Casa di Giulietta
9. Piazza delle Erbe
10. Museo Tridentino di Scienze Naturale

Teatro Olimpico, Verona

Preceding pages **Veneto countryside**

1 Cappella degli Scrovegni

The sky-blue vault studded with gold stars in this glorious Paduan chapel seems to hover over Giotto's vibrant frescoes narrating the lives of Mary and Jesus. The Florentine artist 1266–1337) was summoned by Enrico Scrovegni to work on the chapel in 1305–06, to atone for he sins of his late father, a moneylender. Especially note-worthy of the 38 distinct scenes s the *Last Judgment* on the entrance wall, with ranks of helmeted, haloed and shield-bearing angels. Book in advance and be prepared to wait in the "decontamination" chamber before the 15-minute tour.
◊ *Piazza Eremitani, Padua • Bus Nos. 3, 8, 12 • 049 820 50 06 • Open Feb–Oct: 9am–7pm daily; Nov–Jan: 9am–6pm daily • Admission charge*

2 Bo University

The original lectern where Galileo Galilei held his lessons between 1592 and 1610 can be seen on the guided tour of Padua's historic university, found-ed in 1222 and second only to Bologna as Italy's oldest. The institution boasts the world's first anatomy theatre (1594) where dissections had to be carried out in great secrecy as the church forbade such practices. Other illustrious scholars of the univer-sity have included astronomer Copernicus (1473–1543), Gabriel

Cappella degli Scrovegni, Padua

Fallopius (1523–62), who dis-covered the function of the Fallopian tubes, and Elena Lucrezia Corner Piscopia, the world's first woman graduate *(see p52)*. ◊ *Via VIII Febbraio 2, Padua • Bus Nos. 3, 8, 12 • Guided tours: 3, 4 & 5pm (Nov–Feb 3 & 4pm) Mon, Wed, Fri; 9, 10, 11am (Nov– Feb 10 & 11am) Tue, Thu, Sat • Admission charge*

3 Basilica del Santo

Popularly referred to as "il Santo", Padua's revered site of pilgrimage was built in the 13th century to safeguard the mortal remains of St Anthony, a Francis-can monk and miracle worker from Portugal. Worshippers visit his gleaming tomb, encircled by burning candles, but his tongue is guarded in an intricate reli-quary in the Treasury, recently recovered after being stolen. In architectural terms the basilica blends Romanesque, Gothic, Islamic and Byzantine elements with elegant arched loggias, minarets and domes, and is a treasure trove of art works by Sansovino, Tiepolo and Titian *(see p44)*. ◊ *Piazza del Santo, Padua • Bus Nos. 8, 18 • Open 6:30am–7pm daily • Free*

Basilica del Santo, Padua

Romeo and Juliet

There is no doubt that the Capulet and Montague families existed, though they were probably more friendly than William Shakespeare made out in his tragic 1594–5 play. However the world's most famous star-crossed lovers may actually have come from Vicenza, home town of Luigi Da Porto, author of the original 1530 account.

4 Piazza dei Signori

In addition to the cafés in Vicenza's main square, come to admire the buildings by local son Palladio, whose 16th-century designs shaped both his home town and architecture worldwide *(see p45)*. The basilica boasts twin levels of colonnaded arches, opposite his Loggia del Capitaniato. A statue of the architect stands at the western end of the basilica. ◎ *Basilica Palladiana: • Piazza dei Signori, Vicenza 3600 • Open 9am–5pm Tue–Sun • Admission charge*

5 Teatro Olimpico

A castle courtyard draped with creepers was chosen for this Vicenza theatre, designed by Palladio and completed by his disciple Vincenzo Scamozzi. The performing area is based on a Roman model, while the stage scenery is a replica of the city of Thebes, built for the inaugural play, Sophocles' *Oedipus Rex*, in 1585. Scaled statues and varying stage levels create clever tricks of perspective. ◎ *Piazza Matteotti 11, Vicenza • Open 9am–5pm Tue–Sun (Jul–Aug: 9am–7pm) • Admission charge*

6 Palazzo Leoni Montanari

This lavishly decorated Baroque palace in Vicenza has been newly opened to the public by a banking group. On its entrance portal are carvings of writhing serpents and Hercules is shown in the act of slaying the Hydra on the loggia. The *pièces de résistance* include 120 awe-inspiring Russian icons and 14 fascinating paintings by Pietro Longhi illustrating scenes from 18th-century Venetian life and hanging in the frescoed "Room of the Four Continents". ◎ *Contra' Santa Corona 25, Vicenza • Open 10am–6pm Fri–Sun • Admission charge*

7 Verona Arena

This massive Roman amphitheatre from the 1st century AD is elliptical in shape and measures almost 140 m (460 ft) in length. The arcades and 44-level tiered seating for 22,000 people, that once rang with the cries of gladiator fights, now echo with exquisite arias from operas during the popular summer festival. Verdi's *Aïda* marked the inauguration in 1913, and is repeated every year. ◎ *Piazza Brà, Verona • 045 800 5151 • Open 9am–7pm Tue–Sun (closes 3:30pm on performance days) • Admission charge*

8 Casa di Giulietta

Tourists flock to "Juliet's House", the 13th-century presumed abode of the Shakespearean heroine. Complete with a pretty balcony (added in 1928...) the romantically inclined can imagine her uttering that immortal cry: "Romeo, Romeo, wherefore art thou

Piazza dei Signori, Vicenza

Piazza delle Erbe, Verona

Romeo?" The courtyard walls are plastered with multilingual graffiti left by lovers from all over the world. ◎ *Via Cappello 23, Verona • Open 9am–7pm Tue–Sun • Admission charge*

Piazza delle Erbe
9 Originally Verona's Roman forum, this picturesque square is still a great place for discussing business over a coffee. Parasols shade souvenirs at the animated market, watched over by a winged lion atop a column, vestige of Venetian domination. The 84-m (275-ft) Torre Lamberti offers great city views. ◎ *Torre dei Lamberti, Cortile Mercato Vecchio, Verona • Open 9am–7pm Tue–Sun • Admission charge*

Museo Tridentino di Scienze Naturale
10 Gigantic ferns, weird fish and a crocodile can be admired at this Natural History Museum, all in fossilized form from the Eocene era, 50 million years ago. The treasures hail from Bolca in the Lessini foothills and testify to the tropical shallows that spread across the area prior to the formation of the Alps. ◎ *Lungadige Porta Vittoria 9, Verona • Open 9am–7pm Mon–Thu, Sat; 2–7pm Sun (Jul–Aug: 9am–2pm daily) • Admission charge*

A Day Out in Verona

Morning

🕐 Where better to begin than the inspiring **arena**, where wild animals once made a meal of gladiators as entertainment? Afterwards, relax in the sun with a creamy coffee at Liston 12 Caffè and dig into a freshly baked jam-filled croissant *(Piazza Brà 12, Verona • 045 803 1168)*.

A short stroll leads past the boutiques in traffic-free Via Mazzini, paved with pink-tinged local limestone embedded with ammonite fossils, to **Casa di Giulietta** to the right, or **Piazza delle Erbe** and its elegant palaces to the left.

Backtrack to Via Mazzini for lunch at Ristorante Greppia *(Vicolo Samaritana 3, Verona • 045 800 4577)* for *bollito misto* (nine types of boiled meat) served with a traditional peppery sauce.

Afternoon

To digest lunch, head over the Adige River via the ancient Ponte di Pietra to the Roman theatre on Via Regaste Redentore – well worth a visit even if you're not in town for a summer evening performance. Then follow the river or walk back through town and west towards the medieval Ponte Scaligero, part of the adjoining castle. The triple-arched construction was blown up by the German army in World War II, then rebuilt brick by brick by the town.

The bridge leads to Castelvecchio for a timely apéritif at Barbar *(Via Roma 35, Verona • 045 803 4418)*. Sip a glass of Soave while admiring the fortified walls.

Left **Villa Valmarana** Right **Villa Rotonda**

🔟 Veneto Villas

1 Villa Barbaro

The best preserved villa (1560) by Palladio *(see p45)* lies close to the pretty hilltown of Asolo. This charming country house features all manner of Roman-inspired elements, from the nymphaeum and grotto to the circular temple akin to the Pantheon. Playful *trompe l'oeil* frescoes by Veronese *(see p44)* adorn the main rooms alongside elaborate stucco work, while the garden is punctuated with Classical statuary. Drop in to the estate's wine cellar next door.

⬥ *Via Cornuda 6, Maser, bus from Treviso railway station • Open Mar–Oct: 3–6pm Tue, Sat, Sun & public hols; Nov–Feb: 2:30–5pm Sat, Sun & public hols • Admission charge*

2 Villa Pisani – La Nazionale

A splendid two-floor 18th-century villa designed for Doge Alvise Pisani, with 114 sumptuously furnished rooms and an impressive ballroom decorated by Tiepolo *(see p44)*. Above the huge façade columns, scores of statues line the roof overlooking inner courtyards and a spacious park where the Venetian nobility would promenade on summer evenings. Be sure to try out the wonderful 1721 circular maze. The guest list has included one-time proprietor Napoleon, Russian, Austrian and Swedish royalty, Mussolini and Hitler. ⬥ *Via Doge Pisani 7, Strà • Villa & park: open 9am–6pm Tue–Sun; maze: open Apr–Oct • Admission charge*

3 Villa Valmarana "Ai Nani"

Known for the jaunty statues of dwarfs on the garden wall, these cosy twin buildings stand on a pretty ridge looking up to Monte Berico and its sanctuary. The Tiepolo father and son fresco team were invited here by Count Valmarana in 1757, the former to decorate the main part, the latter the Foresteria guest quarters.

⬥ *Via dei Nani 2–8, Vicenza • Open 15 Mar–5 Nov: 10am–noon, 2:30–5:30pm Wed–Thu, Sat–Sun • Admission charge*

4 Villa Valmarana "La Rotonda"

Perfectly proportioned imposing villa with four temple façades on a hill overlooking the architect Palladio's home town of Vicenza. The house has been imitated throughout the world. It served as the backdrop for Joseph Losey's 1979 film version of *Don Giovanni*. If you want to visit the gilded stuccoed and domed villa as opposed to the rather limited grounds, time your visit carefully as it's only open one day per week. ⬥ *Via Rotonda 29, Vicenza (bus No. 8) • Open 15 Mar–4 Nov: garden 10am–noon, 3–6pm Tue–Sun; villa 10am–noon, 3–6pm Wed • Admission charge*

5 Villa Foscari "La Malcontenta"

Wonderful dignified residence set on the bend of the Brenta Canal, though now rather too close to the Marghera industrial area. Designed by Andrea Palladio in 1571, it is one of his

Left **Villa Foscari** Right **Villa Emo**

most famous creations, with a Greek temple façade, while the interior glows with allegorical frescoes. The name is a reference to the "discontent" of a female member of the Foscari family, exiled here for adulterous behaviour. ◈ *Via dei Turisti 11, Malcontenta • Open Apr–Oct: 9am–noon Tue, Sat • Admission charge*

Villa Barbarigo
The Euganean Hills are the perfect setting for this Baroque garden, designed for the Barbarigo family from Venice by Luigi Bernini, architect of the Vatican fountains in Rome. The villa, dating from 1669, is a private dwelling, but the 15-ha (37-acre) garden provides a boxwood maze, fountains, fish ponds, statues and hundreds of trees. ◈ *Galzignano, Valsanzibio • Open Mar–Nov: 10am–1pm, 2pm–sunset daily • Admission charge*

Villa Emo
Another of Palladio's light-flooded country residences, this one was commissioned by the Emo family and built around 1560. A harmonious central block is flanked by graceful arched *barchesse* (wings), designed for storing hay and farm tools. The interior has lively frescoes by Renaissance artist Zelotti, also responsible for the Malcontenta villa decorations. ◈ *Via Stazione 5, Fanzolo di Vedelago • Open Apr–Oct: 3–7pm Mon–Sat, 10:30am–12:30pm Sun & public hols; Nov–Mar: 2–6pm Sat–Sun • Admission charge*

Villa Contarini
A horseshoe plaza lined with terraced houses faces the façade of this 17th-century country villa, once the focus for a thriving farming community. A remarkable system of acoustics was invented so that musicians performing in the Sala della Musica on the first floor could be clearly appreciated downstairs. An antiques market is held in the grounds on the last Sunday of each month. ◈ *Piazzola sul Brenta • Open mid-Mar–mid Oct: 9am–noon, 2–6pm Mon–Sat (Jun–Sep: 3–7pm), 9am–noon, 2–7:30pm Sun & public hols; mid-Oct–mid-Mar: 9am–noon, 2–6pm Tue–Sat • Admission charge*

Villa Cornaro
Unusual double-tiered, compact Palladio creation, this one dates back to 1560–70. The façade columns are both Corinthian and Doric in style, with acanthus leaves or scrolls around the capitals. ◈ *Via Roma 34, Piombino Dese • Open May–Sep: 3:30–6pm Sat • Admission charge*

Barchessa Valmarana
Formerly guest quarters, these extant "wings" of a 17th-century villa, whose main body was demolished in 1908. Close by are locks on the Brenta waterway, excavated over centuries to divert the river away from the lagoon and eliminate silting. ◈ *Via Valmarana 11, Mira Porte • Open Mar–Nov: 9:30am–noon, 2:30–6pm Tue–Sun • Admission charge*

Left **Ex** Right **Mercato d'Oriente**

🔟 Veneto Shops

1 Pasticceria Forin
A pastry shop specializing in biscuits named after St Anthony and studded with pistachios, pine nuts and marsala. The *pièce de résistance* is a large bun shaped to resemble the town's domed basilica and flavoured with *amaretto* (almond liqueur). ✎ *Via S Francesco 179, Padua*

2 Sportler
All the top brand names in mountaineering equipment and other sports are available, as well as their own makes at lower prices. End-of-season sales offer wonderful bargains. ✎ *Via Altinate 35/37, Padua*

3 Feltrinelli Internazionale
Browse through the well-stocked shelves of English- and other European-language crime and mystery novels, fiction, travel, classics, children's literature and reference books in this chain bookshop. ✎ *Via S Francesco 14, Padua*

4 Antica Pasticceria di Sorarù
Inviting pastry shop lined with tantalizing almond and chocolate delicacies, and special goodies such as the dove-shaped *Colomba* cake at Easter. ✎ *Piazzetta Palladio 17, Vicenza*

5 Cappelleria Palladio
Hat-lovers' heaven, run by a charming couple with a 40-year passion for millinery in this lovely old-fashioned establishment. In great demand for stylish weddings in the country villas *(see pp126–7)*. ✎ *Piazzetta Palladio 13, Vicenza*

6 Il Ceppo
A gourmet's paradise with mouth-watering take-away dishes, pickles and preserves. Buy a catered picnic with wine or simply a crusty roll filled with Asiago cheese or *sopressa* sausage. ✎ *Corso Palladio 196, Vicenza*

7 De Rossi "Il Fornaio"
A range of pastries and wholemeal breads. Try the *zaletto*, a biscuit baked with pine nuts and sultanas, and of course *Baci di Giulietta* (Juliet's Kisses) – almond paste shaped into pursed lips. ✎ *Corso Porta Borsari 3, Verona*

8 Ex
Fashion clothing, Japanese or French ceramics, twig mats and zany tableware are all available in this design establishment. ✎ *Corte Farina 4, Verona*

9 Mercato d'Oriente
Akin to an exotic museum, this antiques dealer dazzles with Chinese and Japanese marvels, Pre-Columbian pieces and both traditional and contemporary carpets. ✎ *Corso S Anastasia 34, Verona*

10 Upim
Wonderful department store with a good range of casual clothes, cosmetics and home furnishings, in the centre of town. ✎ *Via Mazzini 6, Verona*

Price Categories

For a three-course meal for one with half a bottle of wine (or equivalent meal), taxes and extra charges

€ under €30
€€ €30–€40
€€€ €40–€50
€€€€ €50–€60
€€€€€ over €60

Left **Caffè Pedrocchi** Right **Caffè Dante Ristoratore**

Places to Eat

1 Graziati
Buttery *millefoglie* pastries perfectly accompany a strong sweet coffee as you sit outside on the lively market square. Light lunches are served downstairs. ✆ *Piazza della Frutta 40, Padua*

2 Caffè Pedrocchi
This 1831 Neo-Classical coffee house was long known as the "café without doors" because it never closed. Liberals of the 19th century would meet and argue here, though today, after a renovation, it's rather quiet. ✆ *Via VIII Febbraio 15, Padua*

3 Osteria dei Fabbri
The appetizing menu in this rustic *osteria* changes daily, so you may get grilled Piedmont cheese with polenta or spare ribs with *radicchio*. ✆ *Via dei Fabbri 13, Padua • 049 650 3362 • Closed Sun • €*

4 Osteria al Bersagliere
This refined *osteria* does variations on the area's seasonal cuisine. A local favourite is *Baccalà alla Vicentina*, dried salt cod stewed in milk. ✆ *Via Pescaria 11, Vicenza • 044 432 3507 • Closed Sun • No disabled access • €*

5 Antica Casa della Malvasia
A restaurant with an imaginative menu and a vast wine list. Try the *Bigoli all'arna* (spaghetti with duck sauce). ✆ *Contrada Morette 5, Vicenza • 044 454 3704 • Closed Sun D, Mon, 1st week Aug, 1st week Feb • €*

6 Brek
At the western end of the main street, this great self-service restaurant offers cheap, tasty salads, pasta and meat dishes prepared while you wait. ✆ *Corso A Palladio 10, Vicenza • 044 432 7829 • €*

7 Pizzeria Bella Vicenza
Just off the main square, this great-value pizzeria proudly specializes in seasonal vegetable toppings, such as peas, asparagus, aubergine (eggplant) or red chicory. ✆ *Contrà dei Proti 12, Vicenza • 044 454 6192 • Closed Mon D, Tue • No disabled access • €*

8 Caffè Dante Ristoratore
This stylish café can be found in a quiet historic square surrounded by graceful palaces. The place to be seen, sipping tea amid potted palms and cane chairs. ✆ *Piazza dei Signori, Verona*

9 Brek
Right across from the arena, this well-reputed self-service Italian chain restaurant offers a vast variety of meats, cheeses and vegetable dishes. ✆ *Piazza Brà 20, Verona • 045 800 4561 • €*

10 Bottega del Vino
Renowned restaurant that dates back to 1890 and holds 2,500 wines in its cellar. Food-wise, the favourite is *pastissada de caval*, a spicy stew. ✆ *Vicolo Scudo di Francia 3, Verona • 045 800 4535 • Closed Tue • €€€*

Note: *Unless otherwise stated, all restaurants accept credit cards and serve vegetarian meals*

STREETSMART

VENICE'S TOP 10

Left **International Student Card** Centre **Sunbathing, the Lido** Right **Airline ticket**

TOP 10 Planning Your Trip

1 What to Pack

Comfortable walking shoes (not boots) or sandals are essential. You'll be on your feet for a good part of your visit and the stone paving can prove tiring. Bring a bag or case on wheels so that it is easy to get on and off boats and ferries.

2 Passports, Visas and ID Cards

A passport with a minimum five months validity is necessary for nationals of all countries entering Italy. For residents of the EU, USA, Canada, Australia and New Zealand, visas are only required for stays exceeding three months or for those intending to work, but it is always advisable to check with your embassy before travelling. Students should bring an International Student Card (ISIC) for reduced admission fees.

3 Driving Licence

If you plan on any out-of-Venice trips with a rented car, bring a valid driving licence and credit card. Residents from outside the EU will need an International Driver's Licence. If driving your own car, bring vehicle registration papers and full insurance cover. Italians drive on the right.

4 Children's Needs

Young children tire quickly and a fold-up stroller is essential. A backpack child carrier can be worth its weight in gold and can double as a high chair, which are rare in Venice restaurants.

5 When to Go

There's no such thing as a "bad" time to visit Venice. Every season has its attractions, whether that be hot summer days with balmy evenings; melancholic autumn with its fog; crisp winter with the snow-bound Alps as a backdrop, or mild spring with its photogenic sunsets.

6 Public Holidays

In addition to those recognized throughout Italy *(see box)*, the Venice Salute festivity falls on 21 November *(see p62)* and St Mark's Day on 25 April.

7 Time Difference

Italy is one hour ahead of Greenwich Mean Time (GMT), meaning London is one hour behind Venice, the US Eastern Seaboard six hours behind, while most of Australia is nine hours ahead and Japan eight hours ahead. Italy changes to Daylight Saving Time *(ora legale)* from the last Sunday in March through to the last Sunday in October, moving the time difference to GMT plus two hours.

8 Sun Protection

Sunglasses, protective cream and a hat are essential from spring to autumn for pale complexions. Don't underestimate the strength of the sun and remember that there is added reflection from the water.

9 Insect Repellent

Mosquitoes and gnats are a nuisance in summer and few hotels or apartments have protective screening. Should you forget your own, pharmacies stock a wide range of repellents in liquid and electrical form.

10 Electrical Appliances

Italian plugs and sockets entail two or three round prongs and electricity is 220V AC. If you envisage using any appliances bring an adaptor with you, as they're all but unheard of in Venice.

Mosquito repellent and Italian plug

Public Holidays

New Year's Day (1 Jan)
Epiphany (6 Jan)
Easter Monday (variable)
Liberation Day (25 Apr)
Labour Day (1 May)
Assumption (15 Aug)
All Saints' Day (1 Nov)
Immaculate Conception (8 Dec)
Christmas Day (25 Dec)
Boxing Day (26 Dec).

Left **Venice Marco Polo Airport** Centre **Arriving by boat** Right **Tronchetto car park**

🔟 Arriving in Venice

1 Venice Airport

Marco Polo Airport is located at Tessera, 8 km (5 miles) north of the city, on the edge of the lagoon, so arrivals and departures are scenic affairs. Many scheduled European airlines serve the airport including British Airways. Visitors from outside Europe need to fly to Rome or Milan and reach Venice by land. ◈ *Arrivals information: 041 260 9240 • Departures information: 041 260 9250 • www.veniceairport.it*

2 Water Connections

The most exciting way to reach Venice from the airport is by water – the frequent Alilaguna ferries charge about €8. A private water taxi, however, will set you back an vast amount (around €70), depending on time of day and the amount of baggage you have *(see p135)*.

3 Road Connections

To go as far as Piazzale Roma, Venice's car and bus terminal, the cheapest option is the orange ACTV bus No. 5 *(see p135)*, every 20 minutes during the day. Tickets are available from newsagents. Or there's the direct ATVO blue bus tickets available in the arrivals hall).

4 Treviso Airport

Ryanair flies into Treviso airport from the UK and a special bus transports passengers to and from Venice (45 minutes). The airport can also be reached by train from Venice to Treviso, then local bus No. 6, although this route does take longer. ◈ *Treviso airport information: 0422 315 111*

5 By Train

Don't make the mistake of many first-time visitors and get off at Venezia Mestre, but wait until the train has crossed the lagoon for Venezia Santa Lucia Station. The Orient Express is an expensive but memorable way to travel from London between March and November. ◈ *Train timetables: 848 888 088 • www.fs-on-line.com • www.orient-expresstrains.com*

6 By Road

Whether you zoom in to the city via the motorway *(autostrada)* or on minor roads, you'll need to follow signs for "Venezia". Long-distance buses arrive in Venice at Piazzale Roma. ◈ *Road conditions information: 1518 • ACI (Italian Automobile Club) breakdown service: 116*

7 Car Parking

The Tronchetto island car park (€15 for 24 hours) has bus and boat links to the rest of Venice, otherwise it's Piazzale Roma for the exorbitant garages *(parcheggio)*.

More reasonable is Serenissima opposite the railway station in Mestre. The car park and boat terminal at Fusina on the eastern edge of the lagoon is also handy. Never resort to roadside parking – car break-ins are common.

8 By Sea

Daily car and passenger ferries arrive from Greece across the Adriatic and dock at the San Basilio terminal in western Dorsoduro *(see p93)*, equipped with an information office and catering facilities. It also acts as the jump-off point for week-long cruises to the Greek Islands. ◈ *Maritime Passenger Terminal: 041 533 4871*

9 Porters

Porters *(portabagagli)* equipped with trolleys and broad shoulders can usually be found at the maritime passenger terminal, railway station, airport, bus terminal and car park, and at strategic points around town such as Rialto and Piazza San Marco. Rates start at around €1 per item.

10 Left Luggage

Lockers and a left luggage office *(deposito bagagli)* function at Santa Lucia railway station and Marco Polo airport. The Piazzale Roma bus terminal also has a left luggage facility next to the Pullman Bar.

Left **Concert poster** Centre left **Ospite di Venezia** Centre right and right **Italian tourist office logo**

🔟 Sources of Information

1 Tourist Offices in Venice
There are numerous helpful tourist offices around the city *(see box)*.

2 Tourist Offices in the Veneto
Each of the main towns in the Veneto has a tourist information office *(see box)*.

3 AVA Venice Hoteliers' Association
For a modest fee, hotel bookings can be made at a number of AVA offices. ✆ Airport: 041 541 5133 • Piazzale Roma Garage Comunale: 041 522 8640 • Piazzale Roma Garage San Marco: 041 523 1397 • Ferrovia: 041 715 288 • Tronchetto: 041 528 7833

4 Last-Minute Reservations
The efficient VeneziaSì booking service run by the Hoteliers' Association can arrange accommodation on the spur of the moment, free of charge. ✆ 800 843 006 (freephone within Italy) • 041 522 2264 (from abroad) • www. veniceinfo.it • info@ veniceinfo.it

5 Ospite di Venezia
This excellent free magazine published every month in English (as *Guest in Venice*) and Italian by the Hoteliers' Association is distributed at hotels. Crammed with practical details, boat timetables and info on exhibitions and concerts.

6 Wall Posters
Many events in Venice are announced at the last minute by eye-catching posters along the main streets or small versions in shop windows. Get in the habit of reading them for all manner of fascinating local festivities and cultural events.

7 Leo Bussola
The Venice Tourist Board's complimentary glossy three-monthly publication has a detachable pocket-sized programme of exhibitions, concerts and events. Request it for free at tourist offices.

8 Venezia da Vivere
Aimed at young visitors, this slim, brightly coloured booklet printed quarterly by the City Council has listings of what's on, live music, poetry readings, cheap places to eat and shop. Found in bars and shops.

9 Pocket Venice
Another useful free three-monthly bilingual magazine that lists exhibitions, not to mention bars and eateries all around town.

10 Websites
As well as the Tourist Board sites *(see box)*, www.acqualta.com in Italian and English is excellent and has an incredible number and array of useful links for in-depth exploration. Other fairly helpful sites on practical matters are www.meetingvenice an www.aguestinvenice.cor

---

Tourist Offices

Venice
www.turismovenezia.it

Ferrovia S Lucia (railway station) • 041 529 8727

Piazza S Marco 71/f • 041 529 8740

Venice Pavilion • Giardinetti Reali, S Marco 2 • 041 522 5150

Piazzale Roma, Garage Comunale • 041 241 1499

Tronchetto • 041 533 4613

Airport • 041 541 5887

Gran Viale 6, Lido • 041 526 5721 (summer only)

Padua
Piazzale della Stazione • 049 875 2077 • www.padovanet.it/apt

Vicenza
Piazza Matteotti 12 • 044 432 0854 • www.ascom.vi. it/aptvicenza

Verona
Via degli Alpini 9 • 045 806 8680 • www. tourism.verona.it

Left **Venice street signs** Centre **Gondola ride** Right **Vaporetto arriving at San Marco**

10 Getting Around Venice

1 Asking Directions

Whatever your request, a Venetian will nearly always answer *sempre diritto* ("straight on"). The idea is that by following the main flow of pedestrians you'll reach the main sights. A detailed map is always a good idea.

2 Street Signs

Yellow placards point visitors in the direction of the main landmarks such as San Marco, Rialto, Ferrovia (railway station) and Piazzale Roma (bus terminal and car park). But be aware that inconsistencies in spelling may be encountered between street signs and addresses in this guide due to the Venetian dialect applied to local names.

3 Boat Lines

The ACTV runs a marvellous network of public ferries throughout Venice and the lagoon. Buy your ticket beforehand or, if the landing stage is unmanned, ask the crew for a ticket as soon as you board. ➣ www.actv.it for (for routes and timetables)

4 Boat Fares

A one-way ticket can be expensive (around €3, or up to €7 for a family of three). You can get better value from a 24-hour or 72-hour ticket. Children under four years of age travel free on all public transport in Venice.

5 Island Boat Fares

A *laguna nord* day ticket is a good deal for the panoramic circuit via Murano, Burano and its neighbours, as well as Punta Sabbioni (see pp108–111). An equivalent applies for the Lido-Chioggia route (see pp114–17) via a combination of buses and ferries.

6 Season Tickets

If you're staying longer than a few weeks, it's worth investing in a three-year *abbonamento* (travel pass). A passport-sized photo is required. Apply to ACTV at Piazzale Roma or San Marco.

7 Gondolas

Charges are around €60 for 50 minutes with a maximum of six passengers, although this increases after 8pm. The gondola *traghetto* ferry service across the Grand Canal is far cheaper and still spectacular (see p22).

8 Water Taxis

Not exactly a cheap transport option, but it's undeniably stylish to cruise around in a varnished waterborne equivalent of a limousine if you can afford it (see p22). ➣ Consorzio Motoscafi: 041 522 2303 • Serenissima: 041 522 8538

9 Combined City Museum Ticket

The City Museums' combined ticket covers entrance to the Doge's Palace (see pp12–15), Museo Correr including the archaeological section and Libreria Sansovino (see p18), Palazzo Mocenigo (see p82) and the Glass and Lace museums (see pp40–41). The card is excellent value if you want to visit all of them.

10 Chorus Church Pass

If you plan on visiting most of the 15 outstanding churches managed by the Chorus organization, splash out on the all-inclusive combined ticket, rather than paying admission charges for each one. Included among the churches are Santa Maria Gloriosa dei Frari (see pp26–7), Santa Maria dei Miracoli, San Sebastiano and Madonna dell'Orto (see pp38–9). ➣ Chorus: 041 275 0462 • www. chorus-ve.org

Ca' Pesaro museum

For Venice's watercraft **See pp22–3**

135

Left **Official Venice tour guide** Right **Gondola serenade**

🔟 Guided Tours

1 Official Tour Guides
The city's certified multi-lingual guides, catering for individuals and groups, cover every corner of Venice with in-depth history and history of art explanations in some 15 different languages. ⊗ Calle Morosini della Regina, S Marco 750 • 041 520 9038 • guideve@tin.it

2 American Express
An attractive range of walking and gondola sightseeing tours accompanied by qualified English-speaking guides takes place daily. They last for around two hours and can be booked in advance. ⊗ Salizzada S Moisè, S Marco 1471 • 041 520 0844 • www. americanexpress.it

3 Gondola Serenades
If you can't afford a gondola all for yourself, then a group cruise along the romantic canals serenaded by a baritone singing "O sole mio!" is a must. Either reserve through travel agents around the city or ask at the gondoliers' stands.

4 Island Boat trips
Murano, Burano (see pp108–111) and Torcello (see pp30–31) are visited on a four-hour trip in sleek motor launches with a multilingual guide (9:30am and 2:30pm Apr–Oct, 2pm Nov–Mar). Book your ticket at a travel agency or at kiosks in Piazza San Marco.

5 Museum Tours
To get the most out of your visit, join a guided tour run by expert English-speaking staff in the city's many superb museums. Particularly good recommendations are those at the Peggy Guggenheim Collection (see pp34–5), the Archaeological Museum and Sala Sansovino (see p18). Most tours have no extra charge, although a small fee is payable at the Accademia Galleries (see pp24–5), the Jewish Ghetto (see p95) and the Doge's Palace (see pp12–15).

6 Doge's Palace "Secret Itineraries" Tour
In addition to the official parts of the Doge's Palace, these tours take you "behind the scenes", and come complete with fascinating historical anecdotes. Advance booking recommended (see pp12–15).

7 Brenta Villas
This leisurely if rather exorbitantly priced full-day ferry trip across the lagoon sails via the locks on the Brenta Canal to visit a selection of stately villas. Return is by bus. It is run by Il Burchiello in Padua, but can also be booked via Venice travel agents. ⊗ Il Burchiello: SITA, Via Orlandini 3, Padua

• 049 877 4712 • www.ilburchiello.it • end Mar–Nov: Venice to Padua Tue, Thu & Sun; Padua to Venice Wed, Fri & Sun

8 Do-It-Yourself Audio Guide
Easy to operate, the "My Venice Audio Guide" takes you around town with six clearly explained itineraries supplemented by exhaustive historical outlines. They will deliver to your hotel. ⊗ Oltrex Travel Agency, Riva degli Schiavoni, Castello 4192 • 041 524 2840

9 Canoeing Trips
Small group excursions by kayak (no experience required and life jackets supplied) or traditional motor-propelled watercraft are conducted from May to September in the northern lagoon. Full of historical and archaeological highlights along with interesting bird life. ⊗ Azimut, Salizzada S Samuele, S Marco 3148 • 041 520 119 (& fax)

10 Lagoon Boat Trips
Marina Fiorita Viaggi runs full day-trips around the vast northern lagoon area (see pp108–111) with groups of 20–40 passengers in old craft – departures are from Treporti and lunch is usually enjoyed on Sant' Erasmo island. ⊗ Marina Fioriti Viaggi: 041 530 1865 • marinafioritaviaggi@tin.it • May–Sep: Mon–Fri

Left and centre **Venice sales signs** Right **Rialto Market**

10 Venice on a Budget

1 Rolling Venice
A handy pass for 14–29-year-olds entailing holders to a boat/bus ticket that lasts 72 hours, and a range of discounts in hotels, restaurants and shops. It is available from main ACTV ticket offices (see p135) or the Rolling Venice office (Jul–Sep). ○ Rolling Venice: Calle Contarina, S Marco 1529 • 041 274 6 45

2 Accommodation
Sleep cheaply in Venice itself at one of several hostels, otherwise use the camp sites on the mainland or the beach areas – there are cabins or caravans if you don't have a tent (see 151). Crashing out at the railway station is often tolerated though not particularly safe.

3 Public Transport
You can save money by just walking everywhere, unless you're staying at the Giudecca ostel or want to visit the islands. Rather than expensive singles, the boat passes (see p135) or Rolling Venice special deal are recommended.

4 Picnic Supplies
There are wonderful produce markets at Rialto (see pp28–9), Rio Terrà San Leonardo, Campo Santa Margherita (see p32–3) and Via Garibaldi, while supermarkets Standa, Co-op, SU.VE

and Billa are dotted all over town. Cheap wine is dispensed by the litre (vino sfuso) at the many Nave de Oro outlets – take a plastic bottle.

5 Eating out
Italian-style fast food is on at Brek (see p99) or hamburgers at Burger King (see p65) and McDonald's (see p78). For more substantial fare seek out a tavola calda where hot meals are served at the counter and customers sit on stools. Another option is the set tourist menu (menu turistico) in restaurants.

6 Concessions
Children and students with an ISIC (International Students Card) are not the only ones eligible for entry concessions: senior citizens should always enquire at council and state-run museums.

7 Italian Culture Week
Entrance to state-run museums and galleries is free of charge throughout

Italy for the Settimana della cultura, usually in late February or March.

8 Cheap Rail Fares
Outside peak periods, groups of three or more can travel by train as a mini gruppo with Favola Tours, saving around 20 per cent. Other good deals are reduced return fares (R.I.T.) between European cities. ○ Favola Tours: Fondamenta S Lucia, Cannaregio 54 • 041 717 433

9 Shopping
Venice's suburb of Mestre is worth a visit for clothing, shoes and accessories at lower prices than in the city. It also has a huge market on Wednesday and Friday mornings.

10 Bea Vita Laundrette
Save on hotel laundry bills by using this self-service laundrette which guarantees a 45-minute turn-around time. ○ Campiello delle Muneghe, S Croce 6650B

Venetian grocery shop, San Marco

Left **Venetian market** Centre **Mask selection** Right **Street stall**

🔟 Shopping Tips

1 Opening Hours
Food shops open Monday to Saturday around 8–9am, take a long lunch break and then resume business 5–7:30pm, except for Wednesday afternoon when most are closed. In low season clothing and other shops usually close all day Sunday and Monday morning. Glass furnaces (see p64) do not often give demonstrations at weekends.

2 Sales
The official periods for sales (saldi) are mid-January to mid-February then late July to late August. Retailers must show the item's original cost alongside the sale price so customers know how much they're saving. Vendita promozionale is another term for a sale.

3 Tax-Free Shopping
Visitors from non-EU countries can claim a tax refund on purchases that exceed €150 from the one shop. Most shop-keepers will have the appropriate forms – check for the relevant window sticker first.

4 Bargaining
Centuries of commerce have shaped the Venetians into die-hard traders, who feign offence when discounts (sconti) are requested but it's worth a try for cash transactions.

5 Where to Buy Gourmet Delights
Delicatessens and specialist shops are clustered around the Rialto market (see pp28–9), with fresh buffalo mozzarella from the south of Italy, unusual pasta and all manner of delectable ready-to-eat dishes. Supermarkets are also worth perusing for bottled treats.

6 Where to Buy English Books
As well as the Pavilion Bookshop (see p69) and the Libreria di Demetra (see p98), novels and guide books in English and other languages can also be found at Libreria Goldoni and Ca' Foscarina. ◈ Libreria Goldoni: Calle dei Fabbri, S Marco 4742, 041 522 2384 • Ca' Foscarina: Calle Foscari, Dorsoduro 3259, 041 522 9602.

Venice street seller

7 Where to Buy Glassware
It's worth shopping around as many glass shops stock similar items and prices can vary wildly. Murano (see p10) tends to be more expensive than Venice but you get a free demonstration as well.

8 Hypermarkets
Free shuttle buses leave the Piazzale Roma terminal at regular intervals for the huge mainland shopping centres of Panorama, located at Marghera, Carrefour at Marcon and Auchan on the outskirts of Mestre. They're good for everything from groceries through to computers, clothing and sports gear.

9 Street Sellers
Pavement trading is brisk in tourist bric-à-brac as well as imitation designer bags and accessories, with bargaining the name of the game. However foreign visitors should be warned that some countries impose heavy customs fines on imported "fakes".

10 Forwarding Goods Home
Virtually all glass shop staff are experts in packaging fragile and bulky items and they can arrange for forwarding overseas by air or sea. Always check that insurance is included.

Left **Disabled accessibility sign** Centre and right **Wheelchair ramps in Venice**

10 Venice for the Disabled

1 Maps
Ask at tourist offices see p134) for the special map of Venice which shows areas and bridges accessible for wheelchairs clearly highlighted in yellow.

2 Bridges
Cannaregio's Ponte delle Guglie has been fitted with a low stepped rather steep ramp, while four in the San Marco district have a mechanized stair-climber Ponte Goldoni, Ponte Manin, Ponte del Teatro, Ponte dei Frati). The necessary key is available at tourist offices and doesn't need returning.

3 Hotels
Apart from the luxury chains, few hotels in Venice have wheelchair facilities let alone elevators, mainly due to renovation restrictions on historic buildings (which covers virtually everything in town). However a ground-floor room

(camera a piano terra) may be feasible. Addresses can be found in Tourism for all in the Veneto (see "Local Contact" below).

4 Restaurants
Luckily the majority are located on the ground floor though they are not necessarily spacious. Outside dining usually offers easier access.

5 Buses
ACTV bus No. 5, which runs between Piazzale Roma and the airport, is fitted with a mobile platform for wheelchairs and a reserved space with safety straps.

6 Boats
The ACTV vaporetto has a spacious flat area and is easy to get on and off as the landing stages are on the same level as the passenger deck. The motoscafo is best avoided. The Alilaguna launch to and from the airport (see p133) is also wheelchair accessible.

7 Taxis
Waterborne taxis are out of the question unless you can handle steps. However Sanitrans, an efficient private ambulance/taxi service can be booked. The Cooperativa San Marco also has special craft though at a higher rate.
⊗ Sanitrans: 041 513 9977
• Cooperativa San Marco: 041 240 6736

8 Public Conveniences
All of the public toilets in Venice are accessible to disabled users and most are open 24 hours a day.

9 Local Contact
The council-run Informahandicap in Mestre will send you the useful free booklet Tourism for all in the Veneto, as will the Veneto Regional Authority's Tourism Office in Cannaregio.
⊗ Informahandicap: Viale Garibaldi 155, Mestre, 041 534 1700 • Palazzo Sceriman: Lista di Spagna, Cannaregio 168, 041 279 2761

10 Airline and Train Travel
When booking your flight make a request for assistance both on board and at the airport. For trains, railway personnel can aid wheelchair users with a special elevator. Notice of 24 hours is necessary for Italian rail travel and four days for international routes. ⊗ Italian Rail: 041 524 5346

Mechanized wheelchair-climber on a Venetian bridge

vendita biglietti **bus e vaporetti** ticket sale **bus and**

Actv Biglietti Tickets Lire	Corsa semplice Single ticket	Famiglia 3 Family 3	Famiglia 4 Family 4
	6.000 3.10	**45.000** 23.24	**60.000** 30.99

Left **Queues for Basilica San Marco** Right **Boat ticket prices advertised at boarding points**

TOP 10 Things to Avoid

1 Bringing Too Much Luggage
Firstly because it will be a hindrance in this car-less city (you will have to carry it yourself) and secondly because you'll want space for souvenirs.

2 Sticking to the Beaten Track
If you veer away from the signposted – and crowded – triangle between Rialto, San Marco and Accademia, you will most likely find yourself on some deserted but charming canals and get a glimpse of real Venetian life.

3 Clogging up the Streets
People keep to the right here. This habit is of special importance in narrow crowded alleyways to ensure pedestrian flow, not to mention when you're negotiating the raised walkways when the city is flooded.

4 Arriving Without a Place to Stay
Book in advance to save time in queues. E-mail, fax or ring ahead, before you leave home. The touts who assail disembarking train passengers at the station are best avoided.

5 Scams
The Tronchetto Island car park is akin to a "jungle". Don't believe anyone who claims to be a parking attendant (there aren't any) and don't pre-pay a "return" boat ride to your hotel. In Venice itself, don't fall for the "three boxes" betting trick which goes on illegally on bridges.

6 Hidden Costs
Whether ordering a meal or taking a taxi or gondola, it's a good rule to verify all charges beforehand to avoid nasty surprises. Complaints can be addressed to the Tourist Board (freephone 800 355 920). Tipping *(la mancia)* in restaurants is up to personal discretion as a service charge *(servizio)* is generally included in the bill *(conto)*.

7 Buying Goods Without a Receipt
Shopkeepers are obliged to provide customers with a receipt by law and it's also needed if you later decide to exchange an item and for customs when you leave.

8 Entering Churches in Beachwear
Catholic churches no longer require visitors to cover their head, but do still outlaw beachwear, shorts, T-shirts and photographs. Remember they are still places of worship as well as art galleries.

9 Changing Money at Hotels or Shops
For a better rate of exchange, get your money from an ATM (cashpoint machine). Bank tills are also an option but the service can be slow. Don't change too much money at once in case of loss or theft.

10 Getting Stranded
Venice isn't a huge city, but travelling by *vaporetto* can be slow. Allow plenty of transit time to reach the station to catch a train or to keep an appointment.

Alcohol in moderation is part of Venetian life

eft **Public telephone sign** Right **Variety of Italian newspapers**

10 Banking & Communications

1 Currency
In January 2002 Italy joined 11 other European countries by converting its currency to the euro. A transition period will see euros and the Italian lira used simultaneously, but the latter will be phased out after 1 July 2002. Euro banknotes have seven denominations: 5, 10, 20, 50, 100, 200 and 500. There are also eight coin denominations: 2 euros and 1 euro, and 50, 20, 10, 5, 2 and 1 cents. Check on exchange rates against your own currency at the time of travel.

2 Cash Dispensers (ATMs)
Cashpoints are plentiful all over Venice, usually outside bank premises, and allow you to withdraw money around the clock. The logos of the cards accepted are on display. Automatic currency exchange machines with multilingual instructions can also be found in key tourist points.

3 Credit Cards
The most convenient way to carry money and a great help in an emergency. All the major credit cards (MasterCard, Visa, American Express) are widely accepted in restaurants, shops, hotels, and can also be used to obtain a cash advance. Diner's Card is often quoted as the unwanted exception.

4 Travellers' Cheques
Choose a well-known company such as Visa or Thomas Cook, a major currency such as sterling or US dollars, and high denominations as a commission is payable for each transaction. You need to show identification to cash cheques. Keep the receipt and a note of serial numbers separate from the cheques in case of loss. Travellers' cheques in euros are increasingly available.

5 Changing Money
Exchange offices are abundant and usually keep long hours, weekends and public holidays included. Compared to banks they demand a higher commission and give a slightly lower rate but they mean less paperwork and shorter queues. It's worth shopping around to compare rates. Post offices also have exchange facilities.

6 Post Offices
The main Rialto GPO is open Monday to Saturday, 8:10am–7pm, the branch on Lista di Spagna, Monday to Friday 8:10am–6pm, Saturday 8:10am–1:30pm, and the one off Piazza San Marco Monday to Saturday, 8:10am–6pm. Stamps are also sold at tobacconists

Post Office sign

displaying a black-and-white "T" sign. Air mail has been replaced with *Posta Prioritaria* for a faster service.

7 Internet
Internet points have mushroomed in Venice and range from cramped single-computer affairs to flashy modern premises such as Net House, open round-the-clock. Budget hotels are now installing e-mail points as well.
§ *Net House: Campo S Stefano, S Marco 2967-2958 • Map M5*

8 Telephones
There's a public phone on every corner in Venice and pre-paid phonecards *(scheda telefonica)* are sold at tobacconists; remove the dotted corner before use. Dial the zero of all area codes.

9 Press
Newsstands at hot spots such as the railway station and Rialto sell *Time* magazine, several UK newspapers, and the *International Herald Tribune*, which has a daily Italian supplement.

10 TV
Increasing numbers of hotels provide satellite TV for guests so English-language stations CNN, BBC World Service and Sky News are common.

Left **Policemen in Venice** Right **Crowds of tourists**

TOP 10 Security & Health

1 Police
Two police forces operate in Italy. The blue-uniformed *polizia* answer freephone 113 emergency calls, while the military *carabinieri* in red-and-black gear respond to law and order problems on freephone 112. Thefts and serious problems can be reported to either force. ⊗ *Polizia: Fondamenta S Lorenzo, Castello 5053, Map F3* • *Carabinieri: Campo S Zaccaria, Castello 4693/A, Map F4*

2 Pickpockets
Street crime is relatively unusual in Venice but by no means lacking. Pickpockets prey on tourists in crowded places, notably Piazza San Marco and on waterbuses. Put valuables in the hotel safe if possible and don't keep any on show.

3 Consulates and Embassies
Venice itself does not have major embassies in the city apart from the UK consulate, but the nearest Italian consulates and embassies will be able to assist *(see box)*.

4 Lost Credit Cards and Travellers' Cheques
The minute you realize either are missing report it to the relevant number. ⊗ *Visa: freephone 800 877232 (cards); 800 874155 (cheques)* • *American Express: freephone 800* 864046 (cards); 800 872000 (cheques); • Thomas Cook: freephone 800 872050 (cheques)*

5 Women Travellers
Dangerous situations are unusual in Venice as the main streets are rarely empty. However keep away from the Lido beaches at night and stick to busy areas. Chatting up foreign women continues to be a popular pastime for Venetian men.

6 Health Insurance
Visitors from EU countries should be equipped with an E111 form to avoid emergency fees – procedure instructions are on the form. Australia also has a reciprocal health agreement with Italy so the appropriate paperwork is needed. All other nationalities should take out private health insurance.

7 Pharmacies
Seek advice at a pharmacy *(farmacia)* to treat a minor ailment – English is widely understood. Outside shop hours check the pharmacy's door or the local paper *Il Gazzettino* for the night pharmacy roster.

Pharmacy sign

8 Hospitals
Pronto soccorso is the round-the-clock casualty department in hospitals *(ospedale)*, whose staff are usually familiar with the main European languages. Venice's main hospital is the Ospedale Civile. ⊗ *Campo SS Giovanni e Paolo • Map R2*

9 Ambulances
Telephone 118 (free call) anywhere in Italy for an ambulance, including a waterborne *ambulanza* in Venice. Give the name of a prominent landmark nearby to help them locate you.

10 Public Conveniences
These are signposted with a blue-green-white WC logo and are open daily 8am–7/8pm and cost around 50 cents.

Consulates & Embassies

Australia
Via Alessandria 215, Rome • 06 852 721
Canada
Riviera Ruzzante 25, Padua • 049 876 4833
New Zealand
Via Zara 28, Rome • 06 441 7171
United Kingdom
Campo della Carità, Dorsoduro 1051, Venice • 041 522 7207
United States
Via Principe Amadeo 2/10, Milan • 02 290 351

Left **Società Dante Alighieri premises** Right **Glassblowing techniques**

🔟 Studying in Venice

1 Italian Language Courses

Long-established Dante Alighieri holds two- to three-week intensive and half-day courses in Italian language and culture. Students are assisted in finding hostel-type accommodation or rooms with families. ⓢ *Società Dante Alighieri C/O Istituto Tecnico Commerciale Paolo Sarpi • Fondamenta S Giustina, Castello 2821 • Map F3 • 041 528 9127 • venicedantealighieri@ libero.it*

2 University Italian Language Courses

The Ca' Foscari University's language centre offers semi-intensive courses several times a year. Enrolment covers unlimited access to a multimedia lab with audio and video cassettes, DVDs, TV, books and magazines. ⓢ *Centro Linguistico Interfacoltà, Ramo dell'Agnello, S Croce 2161 • Map L1 • 041 524 1642 • www.unive.it/cli*

3 Istituto Venezia Italian Language Courses

Group and individual courses in Italian language and culture are held year-round at the institute, and the school can also arrange family or private accommodation for students. ⓢ *Campo Santa Margherita, Dorsoduro 3116/a • Map K5 • 041 522 433 • www.istituto venezia.com*

4 Watercolour Painting

Spend an intensive week in the open air on a summer watercolour course, or drawing, fresco painting, self-portraiture and printmaking. The internationally known school can accommodate students in its apartments. ⓢ *Scuola Internazionale di Grafica, Calle del Cristo Cannaregio 1798 • Map C1 • 041 721 950 • www.scuolagrafica.it*

5 Restoration Techniques

The Venice European Centre for the Trades and Professions of the Conservation of Architectural Heritage on the island of San Servolo *(see p116)* runs courses in restoration of everything from stone and stucco work to wrought iron and mosaics. ⓢ *Isola di S Servolo, PO Box 676 • Map H1 • 041 526 8546 • www.space.tin. it/arte/carcesar*

6 Glassmaking

At the Murano furnaces learn the basics of traditional blown-glass as well as blow-torch techniques. Week-long or weekend courses. ⓢ *Pandora C/O Materia Prima, Piscina S Samuele, S Marco 3436 • Map M5 • 041 523 3585 • pandora@sorano.to*

7 Ceramics

Small groups are instructed in the art of hand-moulded, wheel-turned pottery and a variety of decorative techniques. Courses commence in March and September, and are held two afternoons a week. ⓢ *La Ciotola, Crosera S Pantalon, Dorsoduro 3948 • Map K4 • 041 526 6127*

8 Italian Cooking

Qualified chef Fulvia starts her year-round cooking courses with a visit to the Rialto market *(see p28)* to familiarize food buffs with the ingredients they will be practising on in her marvellous home. ⓢ *Fulvia Sesani, Ramo del Pestrin, Castello 6140 • Map F3 • 041 522 8923 • fulviasesani@flashnet.it*

9 Mask-making

Starting with the clay mould, you learn to make and decorate a *papier-mâché* mask at the short courses held in the Ca' Macana workshop. For people who don't mind getting their hands dirty. ⓢ *Calle delle Botteghe, Dorsoduro 3172 • Map K6 • 041 277 6142 • www.maskvenice.com*

10 Rowing

Enrol for traditional standing-up style Veneto rowing lessons at this prestigious club. Courses are usually held in spring, though retirees are often on hand to help beginners at other times. ⓢ *Canottieri Bucintoro Zattere, Dorsoduro 261 • Map D5 • 041 522 20552*

Left **Cipriani garden** Right **Excelsior**

TOP 10 Luxury Hotels

1 Cipriani
Set on its own glorious island, the famed Cipriani is a matter of minutes across the water by exclusive launch to Piazza San Marco. It has a private garden with a salt-water pool, and a top class restaurant *(see p58)*. ⊗ *Giudecca 10 • Map E6 • 041 520 7744 • www. orient-expresshotels.com • Closed Jan • €€€€€*

2 Luna Hotel Baglioni
Exquisite service in a sophisticated atmosphere of chandeliers and marble. This is Venice's oldest hotel and hosted Templar knights in the 1100s waiting to embark for the Crusades. Breakfast is served in the drawing room frescoed by pupils of Tiepolo *(see p44)*. ⊗ *Calle Larga dell' Ascension, S Marco 1243 • Map P5 • 041 528 9840 • www.baglionihotels.com • €€€€€*

3 Gritti Palace
Hemingway stayed in this 15th-century palace-hotel located on the Grand Canal. Romantic waterside dining is among the features. ⊗ *Campo S Maria del Giglio, S Marco 2467 • Map N6 • 041 794 611 • www.luxurycollection.com/ grittipalace • €€€€€*

4 Hotel Danieli
While the service leaves much to be desired, the hotel's history *(see p101)* attracts many guests. The best rooms are in the old wing, overlooking the Riva degli Schiavoni. ⊗ *Riva degli Schiavoni, Castello 4196 • Map R5 • 041 522 6480 • www.sheraton.com • €€€€€*

5 Des Bains
This luxurious and discreet Lido hotel has its own swimming pool, tennis courts and private beach area. It also served as the backdrop for Visconti's film *Death in Venice (see p67)*. ⊗ *Lungomare Marconi 17, Lido • Map H2 • 041 526 5921 • www.sheraton.com/ DesBains • Closed mid-Nov–mid-Mar • No disabled access • €€€€€*

6 Grand Hotel Palazzo dei Dogi
With a marvellous garden stretching back to the lagoon, this former convent on a quiet Cannaregio canal is superbly furnished with Murano chandeliers and fabrics crafted by leading artisans. Best value luxury hotel in town with its own guest launch. ⊗ *Fondamenta Madonna dell'Orto, Cannaregio 3500 • Map D1 • 041 220 8111 • www.boscolo.com • €€€€€*

7 Excelsior
Crawling with stars and paparazzi during the summer Film Festival *(see p62)*, this graceful mega-hotel has magnificent rooms right on the beach. A swimming pool and exclusive restaurants are also a feature. ⊗ *Lungomare Marconi 41, Lido • Map H2 • 041 526 0201 • www. sheraton.com • Closed mid-Nov–mid-Mar • €€€€€*

8 Metropole
Majestic good value establishment, immaculately run. On the waterfront only minutes from San Marco, it boasts a wonderful garden, a perfect antidote from the city streets. ⊗ *Riva degli Schiavoni, Castello 4149 • Map F4 • 041 520 5044 • www.venere.it/venezia/ metropole • No disabled access • €€€€€*

9 Europa & Regina
Sumptuous decor in this elegant historic palace right on the Grand Canal, close to the Piazza San Marco. ⊗ *Corte Barozzi, S Marco 2159 • Map P6 • 041 520 0477 • www.luxurycollection. com/europa&regina • No disabled access • €€€€€*

10 Colombina
Timber rafters add atmosphere to the rooms, though the breakfast and reception areas are cramped. On the same canal as the Bridge of Sighs *(see p17)*. ⊗ *Calle del Remedio, Castello 4416 • Map F4 • 041 277 0525 • www.hotelcolombina.com • No disabled access • €€€€€*

Streetsmart

144

Note: Unless otherwise stated, all hotels accept credit cards, have en-suite bathrooms and air conditioning

Price Categories

For a standard,	€	under €100
double room per	€€	€100–€150
night (with breakfast	€€€	€150–€250
if included), taxes	€€€€	€250–€350
and extra charges.	€€€€€	over €350

Left **Casa Cardinal** Right **Hotel Gobbo sign**

🔟 Budget Hotels

1 Casa Cardinal Piazza

Great-value palace guest-house run by friendly nuns and set in a shady garden right on the lagoon edge. Meals available; 11pm curfew. ◎ *Fondamenta Contarini, Cannaregio 3539/A • Map B1 • 041 721 388 • No credit cards • No air-conditioning • No disabled access • €*

2 Archie's House

A bit of a dive but the cheapest backpacker's option in town, close to the San Leonardo market with heaps of cafés and trattorias, and only 10 minutes from the station. Just turn up for a bed and you'll be greeted by an eccentric Chinese-Italian family. Rates get lower depending on the number of occupants for a room and length of stay. ◎ *Rio Terrà S Leonardo, Cannaregio 1814/B • Map C2 • 041 720 884 • No credit cards • €*

3 Alloggi Gerotto Calderan

Handy for the station, with airy rooms, some with bath. Clientele are welcomed by enthusiastic English-speaking staff. Bargain down the rates in low season. Internet point. ◎ *Campo S Geremia, Cannaregio 283 • Map C2 • 041 715 361 • www.casagerotto.com • No credit cards • No air-conditioning • No disabled access • €*

4 Il Lato Azzurro

Great-value lodgings on this garden island where sea breezes are ensured. They arrange canoe trips, bicycles, picnic lunches and half board, entailing mainly vegetarian meals with locally grown produce. ◎ *Via Forti 13, Sant'Erasmo • Map H2 • 041 523 0642 • www.latoazzurro.it • No credit cards • No air conditioning • €*

5 Istituto Artigianelli

On the sunny Zattere, this religious-trade institution keeps its doors open 7am–11pm (midnight in summer). Book well in advance. ◎ *Fondamenta Zattere ai Gesuati, Dorsoduro 919 • Map C5 • 041 522 4077 • centrart@tin.it • No credit cards • No air conditioning • €*

6 Domus Civica

These university rooms are available in the summer months (Jul–Sep). Discounts for students and Rolling Venice participants (see p137). No meals, but plenty of cafés in the vicinity. Closes at 11:30pm. ◎ *Campiello Chiovere, S Polo 3082 • Map N3 • 041 721 103 • No credit cards • No en-suite bathrooms • No air conditioning • No disabled access • €*

7 Al Gobbo

The "Hunchback" is a clean small-scale hotel with a couple of rooms overlooking a bustling square. Easy access from the railway station. ◎ *Campo S Geremia 312, Cannaregio • Map C2 • 041 715 001 • No credit cards • No air conditioning • No disabled access • €*

8 Al Campaniel Guesthouse

Spanish-Venetian couple Gloria and Marco are discreet hosts and offer spotless rooms close to the San Tomà boat stop. Each room has breakfast-making facilities. ◎ *Calle del Campanile, S Polo 2889 • Map N2 • 041 275 07 49 • www.alcampaniel.tripod.com/venezia • No disabled access • €*

9 Instituto Canossiano

A modernized, converted convent with vast courtyards to wander around. Automatic distributing machines for snacks and drinks, otherwise it's not far to the Zattere. There's an 11pm curfew. ◎ *Fondamenta delle Eremite, Dorsoduro 1323 • Map K6 • 041 240 97 13 • cvenezia@fdcc.org • No credit cards • No air conditioning • No disabled access • €*

10 Al Santo

This simple hotel is only a 10-minute stroll from Padua's main sights (see p123). ◎ *Via del Santo 147, Padua • 049 875 2131 • No credit cards • No air conditioning • No disabled access • €*

Left **Locanda Cipriani** Right **Hotel Marconi**

Hotels with Charm

1 Pensione La Calcina

In 1877 Ruskin stayed at this guesthouse on the Zattere, as the friendly staff eagerly explain. Of course, the rooms have been modernized since those days but they have retained their charm and parquet floors. An exclusive street-level terrace overlooks the Giudecca Canal, while another surveys the rooftops. Advance reservations are essential. ◊ *Zattere, Dorsoduro 780 • Map D5 • 041 520 6466 • www.lacalcina.com • No disabled access • €€€*

Pensione La Calcina

2 Accademia Villa Maravege

Book well ahead to stay in this beautiful 17th-century villa near the Accademia *(see pp24–5)*, which was formerly the Russian embassy. Breakfast can be enjoyed in the private garden. ◊ *Fondamenta Bollani, Dorsoduro 1058 • Map L6 • 041 521 0188 • www.pensioneaccademia.it • No disabled access • €€€*

3 Giorgione

A comfortable 4-star hotel with high standards, a warm reception and a pretty garden. Advance booking recommended. ◊ *Calle Larga dei Proverbi, Cannaregio 4587 • Map D2 • 041 522 5810 • www. hotelgiorgione.com • No disabled access • €€€*

4 Ca' della Corte

Charming bed-and-breakfast, where English-speaking Anna will collect you on arrival in Venice, and guide you to these spotless rooms, with all the latest equipment, such as satellite TV. ◊ *Corte Surian, Dorsoduro 3560 • Map K5 • 041 715 877 • www.cadellacorte. com • No credit cards • No air conditioning • No disabled access • €€*

5 Hotel Flora

Though small, the pretty courtyard with creeping greenery is an oasis of calm after the city crowds. Good views from the upper rooms. ◊ *Calle Bergamaschi, S Marco 2283/A • Map P5 • 041 520 5844 • www.hotelflora.it • No disabled access • €€€*

6 Locanda Cipriani

A peaceful, sophisti-cated place on the island of Torcello *(see pp30–31)*, with a list of illustrious past guests. A famed restaurant overlooks a garden and you can explore the island after the day-trippers have left.

◊ *Piazza S Fosca 29, Torcello • Map H1 • 041 730 150 • www.locandacipriani.com • No air conditioning • No disabled access • €€€*

7 Ca' del Borgo

Charming 15th-century villa located on the southern end of the Lido, in an old fishing village. Easy access to Venice and the beach. ◊ *Piazza delle Erbe 8, Malamocco • Map F1 • 041 770 749 • €€€*

8 Hotel Marconi

Popular hotel by Rialto Bridge, with outside seating reserved for guests. Warm reception though simple rooms. ◊ *Riva del Vin, S Polo 729 • Map P3 • 041 522 2068 • www.hotelmarconi.it • No disabled access • €€€ •*

9 San Simon Ai Due Fanali

Tastefully renovated former monastery – rooms feature wooden rafters. Several apart-ments are available. ◊ *Campo S Simeone Grande, S Croce 946/949 • Map K1 • 041 718 490 • www.aiduefanali.com • No disabled access • €€€*

10 Villa Giustinian

An 18th-century villa with a swimming pool, park, magnificent rooms and a fine restaurant. ◊ *Via Miranese 85, Mirano • Map G2 • 041 570 0200 • www.villagiustinian.com • €€*

Note: Unless otherwise stated, all hotels accept credit cards, have en-suite bathrooms and air conditioning

Price Categories

For a standard,
double room per
night (with breakfast
if included), taxes
and extra charges.

€ under €100
€€ €100–€150
€€€ €150–€250
€€€€ €250–€350
€€€€€ over €350

Left **Locanda San Barnaba** Right **Tourist luggage**

🔟 Converted Palaces

1 Hotel San Stefano
Discerning style,
maximum comfort
(Jacuzzi in all rooms) and
breathtaking views. Great
care is taken with details
in this slender tall palace.
⬥ Campo S Stefano, S
Marco 2957 • Map M5
• 041 520 0166 • www.
hotelscelio.sstefano.com •
No disabled access • €€€€

2 San Cassiano – Ca' Favretto
Right on the Grand
Canal, but hidden away in
the maze of alleyways
close to Rialto, is a 16th-
century palace, convert-
ed into a hotel named
after a 19th-century
artist. Elegant rooms
with all mod cons.
⬥ Calle della Rosa, S Croce
2232 • Map N2 • 041 524
1768 • www.sancassiano.it
• No disabled access • €€€

3 Locanda San Barnaba
Minutes from the Ca'
Rezzonico ferry stop, a
quiet, elegant palazzo
hotel, recently refurbish-
ed, with original frescoes
in many of the rooms.
⬥ Calle del Traghetto,
Dorsoduro 2785–2786
• Map L5 • 041 241 1233
• www.locanda-
sanbarnaba.com • No
disabled access • €€

4 La Residenza
In a pretty square
behind the Riva degli
Schiavoni (see p101), a
rather ramshackle but
authentic palace atmos-
phere greets guests. The
rooms are modest but
comfortable.
⬥ Campo Bandiera e Moro,
Castello 3608 • Map F4
• 041 528 5315 • www.
venicelaresidenza.com • No
disabled access • €€

5 Casa Verardo
Beautifully renovated
small-scale palace featuring an atmospheric salon
with antique furniture
where breakfast is served
and a pretty terrace
overlooking a canal. Bar
service and air conditioning units on request.
⬥ Ponte Storto, 4765
Castello • Map F3 • 041
528 6138 • www.
chipsandcolors.com
/casaverardo • No disabled
access • €€

6 Locanda Leon Bianco
Parquet floors alternate
with Venetian terrazzo in
this modest atmospheric
palazzo, in a quiet back-
water just over the
bridge from Campo SS
Apostoli. A couple of
rooms look across the
Grand Canal to Rialto.
⬥ Corte del Leon Bianco,
Cannaregio 5629 • Map P2
• 041 523 3572 •
leonebi@tin.it • No en-suite
bathrooms • No air
conditioning • No disabled
access • €€

7 Albergo Guerrato
Charming old place
at Rialto, saturated with
history and dating back
to 1288. No great views
but heaps of charm and
space. Ventilators are
provided in summer.
⬥ Calle drio la Scimia, S
Polo 240/a • Map N2 • 041
522 7131 • hguerrat@tin.it
• No air conditioning • No
disabled access • €€

8 Locanda La Corte
A relaxing atmos-
phere prevails in this
renovated 16th-century
palace. It once served
the ambassador from
Brescia and is impecca-
bly furnished with period
pieces. Breakfast is
served in the courtyard.
⬥ Calle Bressana, Castello
6317 • Map F3 • 041 241
1300 • info@locanda
lacorte.it • No disabled
access • €€€

9 Villa Ducale
Halfway between
Padua and Venice, this
stately residence stands
in a lovely private park
with statues, while the
beautiful rooms have all
mod cons plus frescoes
and glass chandeliers.
⬥ Riviera Martiri della
Libertà 75, Dolo • ACTV bus
from Piazzale Roma
• 041 560 8020 • www.
villaducale.com • No
disabled access • €€

10 Al Sole
A beautiful place to
stay and convenient for
Piazzale Roma. A 16th-
century palace often
used as a film set, it has
a huge lobby and a court-
yard draped in wisteria.
⬥ Fondamenta Minotto, S
Croce 136 • Map K1 • 041
710 844 • www.corihotels.it
• No disabled access • €€€

Left **Dell'Albero** Right **Locanda Fiorita**

Hotels in Tranquil Locations

1 Hotel Falier
This cheery place is named after the beheaded traitor Doge Falier, "as a warning to guests who fail to pay!" Sunlight streams into the comfortable if small rooms, all with shower, and there's a courtyard dripping with wisteria. *Salizzada S Pantalon, S Croce 130 • Map K4 • 041 710 882 • No air conditioning • No disabled access • €€€*

2 Locanda ai Bareteri
Sergio and Laura are the perfect hosts in their brand new bed-and-breakfast, sandwiched between the Mercerie shopping thoroughfare and a quieter alley. Highlights are old *trompe l'oeil* stained glass, terrazzo flooring and internet facilities. *Calle di Mezzo, S Marco 4966 • Map Q4 • 041 523 2233 • www.venicebedand breakfast.com • No air conditioning • No disabled access • €€*

3 Locanda Fiorita
A very pretty place on a sunny square which was once a public cemetery, off Campo San Stefano. Bargain for cheaper rooms in low season. *Campiello Novo o dei Morti, S Marco 3457/A • Map M5 • 041 523 4754 • www.locanda fiorita.com • No en suite bathrooms • No disabled access • €€*

4 Canada
Fairly ordinary but excellently placed, despite the never-ending stairs. A matter of minutes on foot to both Piazza San Marco or Rialto. Several rooms boast canal views, while others have their own roof terrace. *Campo S Lio, Castello 5659 • Map Q3 • 041 522 9912 • No disabled access • €€*

5 Hotel Dalla Mora
Beautifully located right on a minor canal, this unpretentious but quiet and friendly hotel is only minutes from Piazzale Roma and yet is nice and quiet. It offers clean if not exactly huge, family rooms. *Calle della Madonna, S Croce 42 • Map K2 • 041 710 703 • hoteldallamora@libero.it • No air conditioning • No disabled access • €*

6 Hotel Villa Rosa
Apart from one special room with its own verandah, most rooms rate average in terms of comfort here. However the location is excellent, in a quiet alley close to the railway station. *Calle Misericordia, Cannaregio 389 • Map D2 • 041 718 976 • villarosa@ve.nettuno.it • €€*

7 Due Mori
In a quiet traffic-free street in Vicenza, close to all the main sights *(see p124)*, the Due Mori has spacious spotless rooms furnished in old-style dark timber. *Contrà Do Rode 26, Vicenza (pedestrian zone, 10 mins from station) • 044 432 1886 • No air conditioning • No disabled access • €*

8 Bucintoro
While a bit basic and not terribly friendly in their reception of guests, it's hard to beat the waterfront location at the Arsenale, where all the rooms come with a view. *Riva San Biagio, Castello 2135 • Map G3 • 041 522 3240 • No credit cards • No en-suite bathrooms • No air conditioning • No disabled access • €€*

9 Hotel Canaletto
The great artist Canaletto *(see p44)* lived in this quiet square, only minutes from both the Piazza San Marco and Rialto. Elegant period decor, all mod cons, and several rooms with canal views. *Calle della Malvasia, Castello 5487 • Map Q3 • 041 522 0518 • No disabled access • €€*

10 Dell'Alboro
Located in a relaxing residential area near the Sant'Angelo boat stop, this rather plain hotel nevertheless has rooms with all modern facilities and is very central for Piazza San Marco. *Corte dell'Alboro, S Marco 3894/A-B • Map M4 • 041 522 9454 • No disabled access • €€€*

Price Categories

For a standard, double room per night (with breakfast if included), taxes and extra charges.

€	under €100
€€	€100–€150
€€€	€150–€250
€€€€	€250–€350
€€€€€	over €350

Left **Hotel Marin** Right **Bel Sito & Berlino**

🔟 Medium-Priced Hotels

1 Rossi
Recommended family hotel, high on hospitality. Spotless rooms, many with lovely views, and conveniently placed for Strada Nova. Book well in advance. ◎ *Calle Procuratie, Cannaregio 262 • Map D2 • 041 715 164 • No air conditioning • No disabled access • €*

2 Hotel Marin
Laid-back homely hotel only minutes from both the station and car parks. Many of the bright rooms with pretty window boxes overlook a quiet side alley. ◎ *Calle Chioverette, S Croce 670/B • Map K2 • 041 718 022 • www.hotelmarin.it • No air conditioning • No disabled access • €*

3 Hotel alla Salute Da Cici
Ezra Pound spent time in this 2-star hotel set in the Salute residential area, a stone's throw from the Zattere, not to mention Accademia (see pp24–5) and Guggenheim galleries (see pp34–5). ◎ *Fondamenta Ca' Balà, Dorsoduro 222 • 041 523 5404 • Map D5 • www.hotelsalutedacici.com • No credit cards • No disabled access • €€*

4 Bel Sito & Berlino
A well-placed 3-star hotel facing the Baroque wonders of the Chiesa di Santa Maria del Giglio (see p38). The decor is old style and the atmosphere is warm. ◎ *Campo S Maria del Giglio, S Marco 2517 • Map N6 • 041 522 3365 • www.eurhotels.com/H1478 • No air conditioning • €€€*

5 Al Gazzettino
Centrally located between Rialto and San Marco, this is a basic, decent value hotel. The downstairs walls are papered with sheets from the city's *Il Gazzettino* newspaper, a long-standing neighbour until its relocation to the more practical mainland. ◎ *Calle di Mezzo, S Marco 4971 • Map Q4 • 041 528 6523 • No disabled access • €€*

6 Casa Fontana
Family-managed 2-star establishment in a quiet spot just around the corner from San Zaccaria. Very much a middle-of-the-road place with kitschy decor. ◎ *Campo S Provolo, Castello 4701 • Map F4 • 041 522 0579 • www.hotelfontana.it • No air conditioning • No disabled access • €€*

7 Al Gambero
A guaranteed old favourite on a bridge halfway between Rialto and the Piazza San Marco, wonderful for many sights and shopping sprees. Downstairs is Le Bistrot, a popular nightspot (see p61). ◎ *Calle dei Fabbri, S Marco 4687 • Map P4 • 041 522 4384 • hotelgambero@tin.it • No disabled access • €€*

8 Hotel Kette
Up-market place very popular with a generous buffet breakfast. Several of the fully equipped rooms overlook a picturesque canal. Handy for San Marco and the Grand Canal. ◎ *Piscina San Moisè, S Marco 2053 • Map P5 • 041 520 7766 • www.hotelkette.com • No disabled access • €€€*

9 Locanda Sant'Anna
Despite its dingy appearance, desperate need for maintenance and impossible-to-find location, this guesthouse in down-to-earth Castello is friendly and popular, particularly during the Biennale art exhibitions held every two years (see p62). ◎ *Corte Bianco, Castello 269 • Map F3 • 041 528 6466 • hsantanna@tin.it • No en-suite bathrooms • No air conditioning • No disabled access • €*

10 Hotel Torcolo
You could hardly wish for a more central location than this in Verona, just around the corner from the Arena. Nothing exceptional, but friendly and clean. Guest parking available. ◎ *Vicolo Listone 3, Verona • Bus nos. 11, 12, 13 • 045 800 7512 • No disabled access • €*

Left **Venetian apartment balcony view** Centre & right **Venetian apartment interiors**

TOP 10 Self-Catering

1 Venetian Apartments

This UK company rents out studios, family-size apartments with terraces through to wonderful *piano nobile* floors of luxury palazzos *(see p43)* on the Grand Canal. They also provide plenty of helpful information on practical matters. ✪ *408 Parkway House, Sheen Lane, London SW14 8LS, UK • 020 8878 1130*
• *www.venice-rentals.com*
• *€€€–€€€€€*

2 Veronica Tomasso Cotgrove

Another UK company offers short- or long-term rentals, with a choice of 30 apartments to sleep from two to seven people, and even the chance of a garden, a rarity for Venice. Costs vary depending on location and facilities. ✪ *10 St Mark's Crescent, London NW1 7TS, UK*
• *020 7267 2423*
• *www.vtcitaly.com*
• *€€€€–€€€€€*

3 Carefree Italy

Of their 20 properties available for holiday rents, this UK company includes a lovely apartment in Cannaregio complete with rooftop views. They also arrange for rental of private villas in the Veneto area. ✪ *Radiant Travel Services, Allied Dunbar House, East Park, Crawley, W Sussex RH10 6AJ • 01295 552277*
• *www.carefree-italy.com*
• *€€–€€€€€*

4 Belvedere Italia

A limited but select range of prime properties owned by long-standing families, including a palace near Accademia. ✪ *105 St Peter St, St Albans, Herts, ALI 3ES, UK*
• *01300 34114 • www. belvedere-italia.com • €€€€*

5 Sant'Angelo Immobiliare

Long-established Venice estate agent with 20 fully equipped houses to rent by the week. Several have roof terraces and weekend stays are possible. Services such as cell phone rental and cleaning included. ✪ *Campo Sant'Angelo, S Marco 3818 • Map N5*
• *041 522 1505*
• *www.venicehouse.it*
• *€€€€€*

6 Mitwohnzentrale Venice Alternative Accommodation

Venetian resident Helga Gross is in an excellent position to advise on the 150 fully furnished properties she deals with and will rent you a room or a palace from five nights to up to a year. ✪ *Campo del Teatro Maliban, Cannaregio 5882/A*
• *Map D2 • 041 523 16 72*
• *www.venrent.com*
• *€€€*

7 MyItalianVacation

An efficient US company that manages a vast spectrum of 25 modest and luxurious apartments in Venice with room for up to seven occupants. All are personally inspected. ✪ *3622 49th Ave SW, Seattle, WA 98116, USA*
• *888 465 1460*
• *www.myItalianVacation. com • €€€–€€€€€*

8 Venice Real Estate

The very top in prestigious stately residences. Castles and villas in the Veneto region chosen by Sotheby's, as well as cosy apartments and luxury residences in Venice proper are available. ✪ *Calle Tron, S Marco 1130*
• *Map Q3 • 041 521 0634*
• *www.venicerealestate.it*
• *€€€–€€€€€*

9 Villanet

In operation since 1983, US-based Villanet has 29 places to rent in Venice, some for up to seven people. They can also arrange for car and phone rental. ✪ *11556 1st Ave NW, Seattle, WA 98177, USA • 800 964 1891*
• *www.rentavilla.com*
• *€€€€*

10 Vacanza Bella

Ten prestigious holiday homes are available in Venice itself, most with all mod cons included as well as scenic balconies. Help in the form of cleaning and other services can also be arranged. ✪ *2261 Market St, PMB 281 San Francisco, CA 94114, USA*
• *415 554 0234 • www. vbella.com • €€€–€€€€*

Price Categories		
For a standard, double room per night (with breakfast if included), taxes and extra charges.	€ under €100 €€ €100–€150 €€€ €150–€250 €€€€ €250–€350 €€€€€ over €350	

Left **IYH Ostello Venezia** Right **Ostello Santa Fosca**

🔟 Hostels and Camp Sites

1 IYH Ostello Venezia

Well-run hostel offering cheap meals and a beautiful setting on Giudecca, 35-minute *vaporetto* trip from the railway station (line No. 82) and five minutes to Piazza San Marco *(see pp16–19)*. ⊗ *Fondamenta Zitelle 6, Giudecca • Map E6 • 041 523 8211 • www. ostels-aig.org • €*

2 Ostello Santa Fosca

University student hostel which lets out dorm beds to backpackers, in rambling convent grounds. Cooking facilities are available in summer. ⊗ *Fondamenta Canal Diedo, Cannaregio 2372 • Map C1 • 041 715 775 • www.santafosca.it • €*

3 Foresteria Valdese

A wonderful place to stay near Campo Santa Maria Formosa *(see p102)*, Palazzo Cavagnis is a guesthouse run by the Waldensian and Methodist community and has frescoed dormitories, nice rooms and apartments for families. Advance booking essential. ⊗ *Calle lunga S Maria Formosa, Castello 5170 • Map R3 • 041 528 6797 • www.doge.it/valdesi • €*

4 Istituto Canossiano

Cheap women-only hostel run by nuns on the island of the Giudecca. Closes 9am–3pm then at 10pm

(10:30pm in summer). No meals and cash payment. ⊗ *Ponte Piccolo, Giudecca 428 • Map C6 • 041 522 2157 • €*

5 Camping Fusina

Popular two-star venue for campers and backpackers (in a caravan or under the stars in summer), right on the lagoon edge. Well connected via bus No. 1 from Mestre railway station or the Alilaguna ferry from the Zattere in Venice. ⊗ *Via Moranzani 79, Fusina • Map G2 • 041 547 0055 • www.camping-fusina.com • €*

6 Camping Alba d'Oro

Only 2 km (1 mile) from the airport (bus No. 15), this spacious camp site has a swimming pool, internet point, pizzeria and shops. Tent-less visitors sleep in cabins. Closed November to March. ⊗ *Via Triestina 214/b, Tessera • Map F1 • 041 541 5102 • www.ecvacanze.it • €*

7 IYH Ostello di Mira

This recently opened hostel is located just outside Venice in a lovely country setting. Car parking is available. All linen is provided. Closed October to February. ⊗ *Via Giare 169, Giare di Mira • Venice-Chioggia bus line, Giare stop • 041 567 9203 • www.hostels-aig. org • €*

8 IYH Città di Padova

A bit out of the way, but only a short walk to the main sights and beautifully set in an ornamental grassy square. Cheap meals are supplied. ⊗ *Via Aleardo Aleardi 30, Padova • Bus Nos. 3, 8, 12, 18 or 22 from Venice railway station to Prato della Valle • 049 875 2219 • www.hostels-aig.org • €*

9 IYH Ostello Olimpico

Cheery, helpful hostel close to both the town's main Tourist Office and the Teatro Olimpico *(see p123)*, with meals available at a special low price at a neighbouring bar and restaurant. Internet point and bike hire available. ⊗ *Viale Giuriolo 7–9, Vicenza • Bus Nos. 1, 2, 4, 5 or 7 from the railway station • 044 454 0222 • www.hostels-aig.org • €*

10 IYH Ostello Villa Francescatti

This beautiful 16th-century villa on the hillside above the Roman amphitheatre doubles as the official youth hostel, with dormitory accommodation. It is only 3 km (2 miles) from Verona's railway station. Evening meals are available. ⊗ *Salita Fontana del Ferro 15, Verona • Bus No. 73 (Mon–Sat), 90 (Sun) from the railway station • 045 590 360 • www. hostels-aig.org • €*

General Index

Acknowledgements

The Author

Gillian Price was born in England in 1953 but grew up in Sydney, Australia. She moved to Venice in 1981 and has written books on walking in Italy. Gillian has been contributing to Dorling Kindersley's Eyewitness Travel Guides since 1998.

Produced by Book Creation Services Ltd, London

Project Editor Zoë Ross
Art Editor Alison Verity
Designer Ann Fisher
Picture Research Monica Allende
Proofreader Stewart J Wild
Indexer Hilary Bird
Design and Editorial Assistance
Tamiko Rex, Laura de Selincourt, Jo Ann Titmarsh, Beatriz Waller

Main Photographer Demetrio Carasco

Additional Photography
John Heseltine, Roger Moss

Illustrator Chris Orr & Associates

Cartography Pam Alford, James Anderson, Jane Voss (Anderson Geographics Ltd)

AT DORLING KINDERSLEY:
Senior Editor Marcus Hardy
Senior Art Editor Marisa Renzullo
Cartography Co-ordinator Casper Morris
Senior DTP Designer Jason Little
Production
Sarah Dodd, Marie Ingledew
Publishing Manager Kate Poole
Senior Publishing Manager
Louise Bostock Lang
Director of Publishing Gillian Allan

Special Assistance
Carlo Alberto Albrigo, Tamara Andruszkiewicz, Bruce Boreham, Gianni Nadel, Martin Price, Nicola Regine, Laura Sabbadin, Sally Spector, Venice, Padua, Vicenza and Verona tourist offices, Venice Hoteliers' Association.

Picture Credits

top; tc-top centre; tr-top right; cla-centre left above; ca-centre above; cra-centre right above; cl-centre left; c-centre; cr-centre right; clb-centre left below; cb-centre below; crb-centre right below; bl-below left; bc below centre; br below right.

The publishers would like to thank the following individuals, companies and picture libraries for permission to reproduce their photographs:

AISA, Barcelona: 11b, 20–21c, 52tl, 86-87, 106-107; AKG, London: 31br, 34t, 35b, 50tl, 50tcr, 50tr 50b, © ADAGP, Paris and DACS, London 2001 "The Bird in Space" 1925 by Brancusi 7t, © Succession Picasso/DACS London 2001 "The Poet" by Picasso 34b, ©ADAGP, Paris and DACS, London 2001 "Dressing the Bride" by Max Ernst 34-35c, "Portrait of Vivaldi" by Morellon 52b; Cameraphoto: 11t, 45tl, 45tr, "The Victorious Return of Doge Andrea Contarini after the Triumph in Chioggia" (detail) Paolo Veronese 15b, "Triumph of Venetia as Queen of the Seas" Tintoretto 14b, "Bathing Venus" by Antonio Canova 18b, "Supper in the House of Levi" by Veronese 24-25c, "Portrait" by Rosalba Carriera 25cr, "Mary with Child" by Bellini 44tc, "Portrait of Caterina Conaro" 53b; St Domingie-M.Rabatti: "La Tempesta" by Giorgione 24t; Erich Lessing: 44tl, "Piere di Cadore" by Titian 44tr, "Rio dei Medicanti" by Canaletto 44b; ALLSPORT: 62b; ART ARCHIVE: 15t, 19t, "Enthroned Madonna" by Bellini 7bl, 24b, © DACS London 2001 "The Magic Garden" by Paul Klee 35cr. BRIDGEMAN ART LIBRARY: © ADAGP, Paris and DACS, London 2001 "Studio with a Fruit Bowl" by Dufy 41c. CORBIS: 4-5, 19b, 20-21, 21b, 66b, 70-71, 120-121, 126tr, 130-131, MARY EVANS PICTURE LIBRARY: 50tcl, 51t, 52c, 52tr. LOCANDA FIORITA: 149tr. ESTHER LABI: 128tl. HOTEL MARIN : 149tl MARKA: 62tc, M.Albonico 62tr, Barbazza 115b, 132tc, M.Cristofoti 122tl, D.Donadoni 123b, 126tl, 127tr, E.Lasagni 129tl, M.Mazzola 127tr, M.Silvano 123 tr, G.Luigi Sosso 144tr; MERCADO D'ORIENTE: 128tr; VENETIAN APARTMENTS: all top

COVER: All photographs specially commissioned except: CORBIS: (c) Royalty-Free F/C main image; Michael Dent: F/C b.

All other images are © DK. For further information see www.dkimages.com.

Phrase Book

In an Emergency

Help!	**Aiuto!**	eye-yoo-toh
Stop!	**Fermate!**	fair-mah-teh
Call a doctor.	**Chiama un medico**	kee-ah-mah oon meh-dee-koh
Call an ambulance.	**Chiama un' ambulanza**	kee-ah-mah oon am-boo-lan-tsa
Call the police.	**Chiama la polizia**	kee-ah-mah lah pol-ee-tsee-ah
Call the fire brigade.	**Chiama i pompieri**	kee-ah-mah ee pom-pee-air-ee

Communication Essentials

Yes/No	**Si/No**	see/noh
Please	**Per favore**	pair fah-vor-eh
Thank you	**Grazie**	grah-tsee-eh
Excuse me	**Mi scusi**	mee skoo-zee
Hello	**Buon giorno**	bwon jor-noh
Goodbye	**Arrivederci**	ah-ree-veh-dair-chee
Good evening	**Buona sera**	bwon-ah sair-ah
What?	**Quale?**	kwah-leh?
When?	**Quando?**	kwan-doh?
Why?	**Perchè?**	pair-keh?
Where?	**Dove?**	doh-veh?

Useful Phrases

How are you?	**Come sta?**	koh-meh stah?
Very well, thank you.	**Molto bene, grazie.**	moll-toh beh-neh grah-tsee-eh
Pleased to meet you.	**Piacere di conoscerla.**	pee-ah-chair-eh dee-coh-noh-shair-lah
That's fine.	**Va bene.**	va beh-neh
Where is/are ...?	**Dov'è/ Dove sono ...?**	dov-eh/doveh soh-noh?
How do I get to ...?	**Come faccio per arrivare a ...?**	koh-meh fah-choh pair arri-var-eh ah..?
Do you speak English?	**Parla inglese?**	par-lah een-gleh-zeh?
I don't understand.	**Non capisco.**	non ka-pee-skoh
I'm sorry.	**Mi dispiace.**	mee dee-spee-ah-cheh

Shopping

How much does this cost?	**Quant'è, per favore?**	kwan-teh pair fah-vor-eh?
I would like ...	**Vorrei ...**	vor-ray
Do you have ...?	**Avete ...?**	ah-veh-teh... ?
Do you take credit cards?	**Accettate carte di credito?**	ah-chet-tah-teh kar-teh dee creh-dee-toh?
What time do you open/close?	**A che ora apre/ chiude?**	ah keh or-ah ah-preh/kee-oo-deh?
this one	**questo**	kweh-stoh
that one	**quello**	kwell-oh
expensive	**caro**	kar-oh
cheap	**a buon prezzo**	ah bwon pret-soh
size, clothes	**la taglia**	lah tah-lee-ah
size, shoes	**il numero**	eel noo-mair-oh
white	**bianco**	bee-ang-koh
black	**nero**	neh-roh
red	**rosso**	ross-oh
yellow	**giallo**	jal-loh
green	**verde**	vair-deh
blue	**blu**	bloo

Types of Shop

bakery	**il forno /il panificio**	eel forn-oh /eel pan-ee-fee-choh
bank	**la banca**	lah bang-kah
bookshop	**la libreria**	lah lee-breh-ree-ah
cake shop	**la pasticceria**	lah pas-tee-chair-ee-ah
chemist	**la farmacia**	lah far-mah-chee-ah
delicatessen	**la salumeria**	lah sah-loo-meh-ree-ah
department store	**il grande magazzino**	eel gran-deh mag-gad-zee-noh
grocery	**alimentari**	ah-lee-men-ta-ree
hairdresser	**il parrucchiere**	eel par-oo-ke air-eh
ice cream parlour	**la gelateria**	lah jel-lah-tair ree-ah
market	**il mercato**	eel mair-kah-
newsstand	**l'edicola**	leh-dee-koh-l
post office	**l'ufficio postale**	loo-fee-choh pos-tah-leh
supermarket	**il supermercato**	eel su-pair-m kah-toh
tobacconist	**il tabaccaio**	eel tah-bak-e oh
travel agency	**l'agenzia di viaggi**	lah-jen-tsee-a dee vee-ad-j

Sightseeing

art gallery	**la pinacoteca**	lah peena-ko teh-kah
bus stop	**la fermata dell'autobus**	lah fair-mah-t dell ow-toh-booss
church	**la chiesa**	lah kee-eh-za
	la basilica	lah bah-seel-I
closed for holidays	**chiuso per le ferie**	kee-oo-zoh p leh fair-ee-el
garden	**il giardino**	eel jar-dee-nc
museum	**il museo**	eel moo-zeh-
railway station	**la stazione**	lah stah-tsee- oh-neh
tourist information	**l'ufficio di turismo**	loo-fee-choh c too-ree-smol

Staying in a Hotel

Do you have any vacant rooms?	**Avete camere libere?**	ah-veh-teh ka mair-eh lee-bair-eh?
double room	**una camera doppia**	oona kah-ma ah doh-pee-a
with double bed	**con letto matrimoniale**	kon let-toh mah-tree-mc nee-ah-leh
twin room	**una camera con due letti**	oona kah-ma ah kon doo-e let-tee
single room	**una camera singola**	oona kah-ma ah sing-goh-l
room with a bath, shower	**una camera con bagno, con doccia**	oona kah-ma ah kon ban-y kon dot-chal
I have a reservation.	**Ho fatto una prenotazione.**	oh fat-toh oo preh-noh-tah tsee-oh-neh

Eating Out

...ave you got ... table for ...?	**Avete una tavola per ... ?**	ah-veh-teh oona tah-voh- lah pair ...?
...d like to ...eserve a table.	**Vorrei riservare una tavola.**	vor-ray ree-sair- vah-reh oona tah-voh-lah
...reakfast	**colazione**	koh-lah-tsee-oh- neh
...unch	**pranzo**	pran-tsoh
...inner	**cena**	cheh-nah
...he bill	**Il conto**	eel kon-toh
...aitress	**cameriera**	kah-mair-ee-air-ah
...aiter	**cameriere**	kah-mair-ee-air- eh
...xed price	**il menù a**	eel meh-noo ah
...menu	**prezzo fisso**	pret-soh free-soh
...ish of the day	**piatto del giorno**	pee-ah-toh dell jor-no
...tarter	**antipasto**	an-tee-pass-toh
...rst course	**il primo**	eel pree-moh
...ain course	**il secondo**	eel seh-kon-doh
...egetables	**contorni**	eel kon-tor-noh
...essert	**il dolce**	eel doll-cheh
...over charge	**il coperto**	eel koh-pair-toh
...ine list	**la lista dei**	lah lee-stah day
	vini	vee-nee
...lass	**il bicchiere**	eel bee-kee-air- eh
...ottle	**la bottiglia**	lah bot-teel-yah
...nife	**il coltello**	eel kol-tell-oh
...ork	**la forchetta**	lah for-ket-tah
...poon	**il cucchiaio**	eel koo-kee- eye-oh

Menu Decoder

...'acqua ...inerale	lah-kwah mee-nair- ah-leh gah-zah-tah/	mineral water
gassata/	nah-too-rah-leh	fizzy/still
naturale		
agnello	ah-niell-oh	lamb
aglio	al-ee-oh	garlic
al forno	al for-noh	baked
alla griglia	ah-lah greel-yah	grilled
la birra	lah beer-rah	beer
la bistecca	lah bee-stek-kah	steak
il burro	eel boor-oh	butter
il caffè	eel kah-feh	coffee
la carne	la kar-neh	meat
carne di	kar-neh dee	
maiale	mah-yah-leh	pork
la cipolla	la chip-oh-lah	onion
fagioli	ee fah-joh-lee	beans
il formaggio	eel for-mad-joh	cheese
le fragole	leh frah-goh-leh	strawberries
il fritto misto	eel free-toh mees-toh	mixed fried dish
la frutta	la froot-tah	fruit
frutti di mare	froo-tee dee mah-reh	seafood
i funghi	ee foon-ghee	mushrooms
i gamberi	ee gam-bair-ee	prawns
il gelato	eel jel-lah-toh	ice cream
l'insalata	leen-sah-lah-tah	salad
il latte	eel laht-teh	milk
il manzo	eel man-tsoh	beef
l'olio	loh-lee-oh	oil
il pane	eel pah-neh	bread
le patate	leh pah-tah-teh	potatoes
le patatine	leh pah-tah-teen-eh	

fritte	free-teh	chips
il pepe	eel peh-peh	pepper
il pesce	eel pesh-eh	fish
il pollo	eel poll-oh	chicken
il pomodoro	eel poh-moh-dor-oh	tomato
il prosciutto	eel pro-shoo-toh	ham
cotto/crudo	kot-toh/kroo-doh	cooked/cured
il riso	eel ree-zoh	rice
il sale	eel sah-leh	salt
la salsiccia	lah sal-see-chah	sausage
succo	soo-koh	orange/lemon
d'arancia/	dah-ran-chah/	juice
di limone/	dee lee-moh-neh	
il tè	eel teh	tea
la torta	lah tor-tah	cake/tart
l'uovo	loo-oh-voh	egg
vino bianco	vee-noh bee- ang-koh	white wine
vino rosso	vee-noh ross-oh	red wine
le vongole	leh von-goh-leh	clams
lo zucchero	loh zoo-kair-oh	sugar
la zuppa	lah tsoo-pah	soup

Numbers

1	**uno**	oo-noh
2	**due**	doo-eh
3	**tre**	treh
4	**quattro**	kwat-roh
5	**cinque**	ching-kweh
6	**sei**	say-ee
7	**sette**	set-teh
8	**otto**	ot-toh
9	**nove**	noh-veh
10	**dieci**	dee-eh-chee
11	**undici**	oon-dee-chee
12	**dodici**	doh-dee-chee
13	**tredici**	tray-dee-chee
14	**quattordici**	kwat-tor-dee- chee
15	**quindici**	kwin-dee-chee
16	**sedici**	say-dee-chee
17	**diciassette**	dee-chah-set-teh
18	**diciotto**	dee-chot-toh
19	**diciannove**	dee-chah-noh- veh
20	**venti**	ven-tee
30	**trenta**	tren-tah
40	**quaranta**	kwah-ran-tah
50	**cinquanta**	ching-kwan-tah
60	**sessanta**	sess-an-tah
70	**settanta**	set-tan-tah
80	**ottanta**	ot-tan-tah
90	**novanta**	noh-van-tah
100	**cento**	chen-toh
1,000	**mille**	mee-leh
2,000	**duemila**	doo-eh mee-lah
1,000,000	**un milione**	oon meel-yoh- neh

Time

one minute	**un minuto**	oon mee-noo-toh
one hour	**un'ora**	oon or-ah
a day	**un giorno**	oon jor-noh
Monday	**lunedì**	loo-neh-dee
Tuesday	**martedì**	mar-teh-dee
Wednesday	**mercoledì**	mair-koh-leh-dee
Thursday	**giovedì**	joh-veh-dee
Friday	**venerdì**	ven-air-dee
Saturday	**sabato**	sah-bah-toh
Sunday	**domenica**	doh-meh-nee-kah

Index to Main Streets